# Jesus Christ:
# the witness of history

# JESUS CHRIST:
# THE WITNESS OF HISTORY

## SIR NORMAN ANDERSON

O.B.E., Q.C., LL.D., F.B.A.
*formerly Professor of Oriental Laws,*
*and Director of the Institute of Advanced Legal Studies,*
*in the University of London*

**INTER-VARSITY PRESS**
**LEICESTER, ENGLAND**
**DOWNERS GROVE, ILLINOIS U.S.A.**

INTER-VARSITY PRESS
38 De Montfort Street, Leicester LE1 7GP, England
Box 1400, Downers Grove, Illinois 60515, U.S.A.

Unless otherwise stated, quotations from the Bible are taken from the
HOLY BIBLE: NEW INTERNATIONAL VERSION. Copyright © 1978 by the
International Bible Society, New York. Published in Great Britain
by Hodder & Stoughton Limited, and used by permission of
Zondervan Bible Publishers, Grand Rapids, Michigan.

First Edition 1969
(under the title *Christianity: the witness of history*)
Second Edition (entirely revised and reset) 1985
(under the title *Jesus Christ: the witness of history*)

**British Library Cataloguing in Publication Data**

Anderson, Norman
  Jesus Christ: the witness of history. – 2nd ed.
  1. Jesus Christ – Historicity
  I. Title    II. Anderson, Norman. Christianity
  232.9'08    BT303.2
  ISBN 0–85111–324–9

**Library of Congress Cataloging in Publication Data**

Anderson, J. N. D. (James Norman Dalrymple), Sir, 1908 –
  Jesus Christ, the witness of history. |
  Rev. ed. of: Christianity. 1969.
  Bibliography: p.
  1. Jesus Christ – Historicity.    2. Jesus Christ – Person and offices.
  3. Apologetics – 20th century.
  I. Anderson, J. N. D. (James Norman Dalrymple), Sir, 1908 –
  Christianity.    II. Title.
  BT303.2.A62    1985    232.9'08    84-15703
  ISBN 0-87784-336-8 (U.S.)

Typeset in Great Britain by Nuprint Services, Harpenden, Herts.
Printed by Billing & Sons Ltd., Worcester

*Inter-Varsity Press, England is the publishing division of the Universities and Colleges
Christian Fellowship (formerly the Inter-Varsity Fellowship), a student movement
linking Christian Unions in universities and colleges throughout the United Kingdom
and the Republic of Ireland, and a member movement of the International Fellowship of
Evangelical Students. For information about local and national activities write to
UCCF, 38 De Montfort Street, Leicester LE1 7GP.* 🔲

*InterVarsity Press, U.S.A., is the book-publishing division of Inter-Varsity Christian
Fellowship, a student movement active on campus at hundreds of universities, colleges
and schools of nursing. For information about local and regional activities, write
IVCF, 233 Langdon St., Madison, WI 53703.*

*Distributed in Canada through InterVarsity Press, 860 Denison St., Unit 3, Markham,
Ontario L3R 4H1.*

# Contents

# Preface

'Is it relevant?' is one of the first questions people ask about anything today. This is fair enough, and it should serve as a salutary reminder – whether to the academic theologian in his ivory tower, or to the ordinary Christian in his everyday life – that he must always ask himself if his esoteric theories, or his routine repetition of traditional doctrines, will be of any practical value to the great majority of his contemporaries.

Why, then, should this book be concerned primarily with the first rather than the twentieth century? Are the events of nearly two thousand years ago really so vitally important to us today? Whatever the theoretical importance of these events, moreover, are they in point of fact credible to the modern mind? Should not Christianity be judged today more in terms of the moral impact of its ethical teaching on our own immediate problems – or, perhaps, in terms of the comfort and encouragement it still demonstrably brings to some of those teeming millions who have to face the dismal squalor of inner-city life, the near despair of continued unemployment, or the futility of a rat-race which still absorbs so much of our lives in spite of the ever-present menace of a nuclear holocaust? In a word, should not Christianity be evaluated today by criteria from ethics and experience, rather than those of history?

In this context it is vital to remember that the Christian faith did not emerge from some popular legend (largely based, like most of those mystery religions which preceded, accompanied or followed the advent of Christ, on the phenomena of nature), nor yet from any process of metaphysical speculation. It owed its origin to a life that was really lived and a death that was really died by a fully historical person about whom we have documentary evidence recorded while many of those who knew him intimately were still alive. Incredible though it may seem, these people unite in their testimony not only about his life, teaching and death, but in their assertion that he was raised again from the dead – and their testimony is supported by a wealth of circumstantial evidence.

Certainly the Christian faith rests squarely on existential, as well as historical, criteria. Records could be multiplied of persons who, like the man born blind of whom we read in John 9, have met the cynicism, contempt and persecution of hostile critics by the simple testimony: 'One thing I do know: I was blind but now I see.' And one unforgettable experience on the Damascus road was enough to change Saul the Pharisee from his implacable hostility to a faith he regarded as completely untenable into Paul the apostle whose testimony no hardship, suffering or violence could silence.

But existential evidence is not enough by itself. There must be a credible basis for the alleged experience if it is to be meaningful to others; and its contents and results must be such that they can be assessed and tested by some objective criteria.

I well remember the day when a Muslim Professor in Cairo, a recognized authority on Islamic history, told me that religion, in his view, was not to be approached so much as a matter of science as of art. When I asked him what he meant, he explained that in a scientific monograph the strict accuracy of all the relevant facts is of fundamental importance, whereas in a poem the vital point is the aesthetic impact of the composition as a whole, rather than the factual accuracy of every detail. Similarly, in matters of religion, the criterion is not whether the facts on which Christianity, Islam or any other faith is said to rest will stand up to scholarly criticism, but whether the religion concerned makes its adherents feel more 'fulfilled' in themselves and more kindly disposed to others.

I replied – rather flippantly, I fear – that when I was a boy at school we played a football match against what was then called a lunatic asylum (and I could vividly remember being locked in while we changed our clothes, so that we should not get mixed up with the other team!). We were told, I recall, that one of the patients in that asylum firmly believed that he was a poached egg, and went about every day begging for a piece of toast to sit on. If he was given this, he at once became contented and amenable, while if it was withheld he remained unhappy and fractious. But I could hardly believe that my Muslim friend would regard 'fulfilment' of this sort as meeting his criteria for an adequate religion!

This is a somewhat absurd illustration. But it is obvious that beliefs based on purely existential criteria, even though held by much more normal and rational people, may equally prove to be ill-founded. They may sustain a person for as long as he believes them; but his disappointment and disillusionment when he comes to realize they are false will be in direct proportion to the fervour of his former conviction. And if a person were sustained through life by a conviction which concerns not only time but eternity, only to find at the end that it was an illusion and a mockery, that would be stark tragedy.

C. S. Lewis tells a story of an officer in the RAF who, after listening to a talk on Christianity, burst out with the protest: 'I've no use for all that stuff. But, mind you, I'm a religious man too. I know there's a God. I've felt Him: out alone in the desert at night: the tremendous mystery. And that's just why I don't believe all your neat little dogmas and formulas about Him. To anyone who's met the real thing they all seem so petty and pedantic and unreal!' And Lewis remarks that, in a sense, he quite agreed with that man. He may well have had a real experience of some sort in the desert, and 'when he turned from that experience to the Christian creeds, I think he really was turning from something real to something less real'.

'In the same way,' Lewis writes, 'if a man has once looked at the Atlantic from the beach, and then goes and looks at a map of the Atlantic, he also will be turning from something real to something less real: turning from real waves to a bit of coloured paper. But here comes the point. The map is admittedly only coloured paper, but there are two things you have to remember about it. In the first place, it is based on what hundreds and thousands of people have found out by sailing the real Atlantic. In that way it has behind it masses of experience just as real as the one you could have from the beach; only, while yours would be a simple isolated glimpse, the map fits all those different experiences together. In the second place, if you want to go anywhere, the map is absolutely necessary. As long as you are content with walks on the beach, your own glimpses are far more fun than looking at a map. But the map is going to be more use than walks on the beach if you want to get to America' (Lewis, *Mere Christianity*, pp.121f.).[1]

It seems obvious, then, that the existential experiences of any one individual can be regarded as having no more than a subjective value for himself alone, unless they can be tested and compared with those of others. But it is often asserted today that such experiences are, in their very nature, incommunicable. Francis Schaeffer writes that Karl Jaspers, for example, lays a great deal of emphasis on the need to wait for a non-rational 'final experience' which would give meaning to life. People who follow Jaspers have come to Schaeffer and said 'I have had a final experience', but they never expected him to ask them what it was. If he did, it would prove that he was not among the initiated. The very fact that it was an *existential* experience meant that it could not be communicated. Such people sometimes recognized, it seems, that Schaeffer himself had had a 'final experience' and commented on this fact; but when he told them that his experience *could* be verbalized and rationally discussed, they replied that this was impossible, and that he was trying to do something that cannot be done (Schaeffer, pp.22f.).

It is basic to the Christian experience, however, not only that it can be expressed in words – however inadequately – and compared with that of others, but that it is directly

---

[1] Reference to other books and sources is given in abbreviated form, using the author's name only, or author and title where there are two or more works by the same author quoted in this present volume. Full bibliographical details are given in the Bibliography (pp.165ff.)

concerned with the Christ who was born in Bethlehem, taught in Galilee and Judaea and died outside the walls of Jerusalem nearly two thousand years ago. Christians, of course, believe – with the first disciples – that he rose again and is a living Saviour with whom they can have an existential encounter, and a continuing fellowship, today. But unless the one with whom they have this 'encounter' is the very same Christ about whom the Gospels speak, the encounter they claim to have had is not authentically Christian. It is fatally easy for the human mind to construct a 'Jesus' of its own imagining.

This is why it is essential to go back to the first century and consider the phenomena presented by the New Testament, as we shall attempt to do in this book. First, we shall examine the historical basis on which the whole Christian revelation rests and ask ourselves whether it is convincing. Next, we shall concentrate on the person of Christ as depicted in the Gospels and try to make up our minds, on the evidence, what conclusion we must reach about him. Then we shall turn our attention to his death on a Roman gibbet and consider whether this was in fact inevitable and how it should be understood. Finally, we shall weigh the evidence for the empty tomb and risen Lord of the New Testament testimony and try to decide whether this rests on fact or fancy, on historical event or mythological reconstruction.

Professor C.F.D. Moule, in *The Phenomenon of the New Testament,* quotes D. E. Jenkins' remark that 'Christianity is based on indisputable facts...I do not say that Christianity is the indisputable interpretation of these facts' (*Jesus and God*) and then proceeds: 'It is precisely some of these indisputable facts that I here present, asking whether the Christian interpretation, though I agree that it is not indisputable, is not by far the most plausible – almost (I would venture to think) the inescapable – interpretation' (p.3).

It is true, as Moule observes, that 'rational conviction, even when it can be had, is very different from commitment... Commitment to Christ is a matter for the entire person, not for his mind alone; and intellectual conviction (if, indeed, it can be had at all without the whole person being involved) is not the whole business. But the whole business, precisely because it concerns the whole person, can never be achieved in defiance of the intellect. Reason, though not the whole, is part of the personal response' (pp.5f.). Indeed, intellectual conviction constitutes, in a very real sense, the essential basis for the self-commitment of any rational and moral being, made in the 'image', of his Creator.

But where is such intellectual conviction to be found? The essence of the sense of frustration and despair which seems to characterize contemporary thought is the denial that basic questions about God, man and human destiny can ever receive an authoritative answer. It is to such that the Jesus of the New Testament furnishes what Carnegie Simpson terms 'the most patent and accessible of data'. What are these data? Not metaphysical ideas or unverifiable sentiments, but data concerned with a historical person, who constitutes 'a fact as available as any other fact'. And he pertinently asks how many of those who assume an agnostic attitude to religion have honestly brought their minds and hearts and consciences face to face with the fact of Christ, and candidly considered if it means anything to them for religion. 'It is impossible to say that no one has the right to be an agnostic. But no one has the right to be an agnostic till he has thus dealt with the question,' and faced this fact with an open mind. 'After that, he may be an agnostic – if he can' (Simpson, pp.8f.)

# 1
# The historical basis: is it convincing?

*The fundamental criterion · Christianity: its unique claims · Extra-biblical evidence · The New Testament evidence· The biblical Christ and the historical Jesus · History confirmed by experience · A greatly exaggerated gap · Some examples of the apostolic proclamation · The reliability of the apostolic witness · How Jesus himself authenticates the Gospels · The apocryphal Gospels · My own stance in this book*

## The fundamental criterion

We live in an age of comparative studies. In part this is probably an almost inevitable reaction against the narrow specialization in reading and research to which the vast output of contemporary scholarship condemns most of us; but it also represents a recognition of the light which other systems of law, political theory or religion can throw on our own.

In the sphere of religion this impulse has been inspired by a new spirit of sympathy and understanding, which is greatly to be welcomed. But it has resulted, all too often, in an unprecedented attitude of personal detachment, which certainly makes an objective evaluation of data somewhat easier, but may well make any first-hand experience of faith correspondingly more difficult.

Religions can, of course, be compared at a number of different levels. We can make a comparative study of the philosophy which lies behind them, or the theological teaching which is peculiar to each. We can compare their ethical demands, their liturgical legacy, their historical development, their missionary enthusiasm or their impact on the thought and conduct of their adherents. All these different approaches are eminently relevant to a comparative study of Christianity as one among the world's great religions.

It seems to me inescapable, however, that anyone who chanced to read the pages of the New Testament for the first time would come away with one overwhelming impression – that here is a faith that 'does not understand itself to be the discovering and imparting of generally valid, timeless truths', but that is firmly based on certain allegedly historical events – a faith which would be false and misleading if those events had not actually taken place, but which, if they did take place, is unique in its relevance and exclusive in its demands on our allegiance. For these events did not merely set a

> process in motion and then themselves sink back into the past. The unique, historical origin of Christianity is ascribed permanent, authoritative, absolute significance: what happened once is said to have happened once for all and therefore to have continuous efficacy . . . . From the beginning, theology has been faced with the task of comprehending and expressing the event of revelation in such a way that its two-fold characteristics are preserved: its historicity and its character as revelation, its once-for-all-ness as an historical event and its permanent immediacy (Zahrnt, pp.27f.)

This assessment of the Christian faith, however, has been challenged from two different angles. First, there are many today from inside the tradition of Christendom who would question, in varying degrees, the historical basis on which the message of the New Testament is founded. Secondly, there are others, both from inside and outside the tradition, who would deny that Christianity, whatever its basis in history, can be regarded as unique in its authority or final in its claims.

Those who question the historical events which the New Testament consistently postulates as the genesis, foundation and content of the Christian message do not, of course, doubt the historical phenomenon of the eruption of the Christian faith on the Graeco-Roman world, the joy and spontaneity of the early Christians, or even – in the vast majority of cases – the fact that the Jesus to whom they attributed their faith was no figment of their imagination. It is true that a few isolated individuals have tried to dismiss the unique figure which dominates the New Testament as a beautiful myth; and this attitude, as adopted by Karl Marx, has become widespread in Communist thinking. But it has been justly remarked that the arguments put forward to support this theory 'have again and again been answered and annihilated by first-rank scholars' (Dunkerley, p.12).

More recently, John Allegro has, on different occasions, suggested that the Christ of the Gospels was a mere reflection or reconstruction of the 'Teacher of Righteousness' who inspired the community of the Dead Sea Scrolls[1] – a suggestion which has been decisively refuted by a galaxy of experts[2] – and has even made the wild assertion that the very name 'Jesus' was a code-word for the cult of the 'sacred mushroom'. Somewhat more soberly than this, around the turn of the century the theory of the 'Christ myth' had been propounded, with the suggestion that 'there had never been a real Jesus of Nazareth and that the basis of the Christ

[1] In a lecture given at Richmond on 29 March 1968, Allegro himself apparently indicated that he had now come to see that the Teacher of Righteousness could not bear the burden of explaining away Christianity! But he still, it seems, permitted himself asides such as 'if we suppose for a fleeting moment that John the Baptist existed...' and 'if Jesus existed...' (*cf. The Christian and Christianity Today*, 12 April 1968, p.28). Yet in his scholarly work *Search in the Desert* he has acknowledged that '....the real issues have been overlaid too often by special pleading in attempts to prove the falsity or truth of Christianity on the basis of new evidence. The Scrolls do neither. The light they have brought has been upon the immediate background of Christianity, in particular, the kind of Judaism from which Christianity probably evolved' (p.173).

[2] *Cf.* the letter published in *The Times* on 21 December 1965 from Professors G. R. Driver, H. H. Rowley, Peter R. Ackroyd, Matthew Black, J. B. Segal, D. Winton Thomas, Edward Ullendorff and D. J. Wiseman, stating that 'Nothing that appears in the Scrolls hitherto discovered throws any doubt on the originality of Christianity...nor is there any hint that the Righteous Teacher may have been regarded as in any sense divine'. As for Allegro's wild theorizing in *The Sacred Mushroom and the Cross*, this has been dismissed by fifteen experts in Semitic languages and related fields, in a letter published in *The Times* on 26 May 1970, as 'not based on any philological or other evidence that they can regard as scholarly' – and has met with scathing criticism in review after review.

of the New Testament was a mythical, supra-historical figure to whom Christians had subsequently given a time and place, thus artificially historicizing him'. But it was not difficult, as Otto Betz promptly added, for New Testament scholars like Bousset, Jülicher or Klostermann 'to expose the "Christ myth" as a phantom', and since that time, he asserts, 'no serious scholar has ventured to postulate the non-historicity of Jesus' (Betz, p.9). So it is, I think, true to say that the vast majority of both scholars and laymen would concur with James Frazer's magisterial statement that 'The doubts which have been cast on the historical reality of Jesus are, in my judgment, unworthy of serious attention' (*The Golden Bough*, Vol. IX, p.412n.). After all, why did all the contemporary Mystery religions die out, and Christianity alone survive? There is one obvious answer. It was because the cults were based on myths, while Christianity owed its origin to a real person who could really save.

No, it is not the historical reality of Jesus himself which is seriously in doubt today – although to this we must subsequently return – but rather the historicity of what is said about him in the New Testament and the relevance or irrelevance of such historicity. The teaching of the apostolic church about the person and work of Jesus can, of course, scarcely be called in question, for to this the New Testament bears unequivocal witness. The point at issue is how far this teaching can be explained in terms of a mythology which reflects and symbolizes the subjective belief and experience of the apostles and their followers rather than the objective, historical facts on which that belief and experience were allegedly founded. It has even been suggested that historical factuality is irrelevant in this context except for the most minimal anchoring in history of the summons to decision, and that all that matters is that men and women can still come to the same basic experience which the early church expressed in these mythological terms. Faith, it is claimed, needs only the most tenuous links with history.

But this seems strangely alien to the attitude of the New Testament writers themselves. That attitude can, I think, best be summarized in Paul's categorical assertion that 'if

Christ was not raised then neither our preaching nor your faith has any meaning at all. Further it would mean that we are lying in our witness for God, for we have given our solemn testimony that he did raise up Christ' (1 Corinthians 15:14f., JBP). Nor was this testimony confined to any vague or general affirmation that the crucified Christ had been exalted and glorified; it included explicit reference to several of the resurrection appearances, and an implicit reference to the empty tomb (*cf.* pp.120–125, below). And the significance of this passage lies not only in the fact that it is so unequivocal and clear-cut, but that it comes in an Epistle whose Pauline authorship and very early date are accepted by every reputable scholar (*cf.* pp.120f., below).

The same fundamental attitude, however, underlies the whole New Testament. The Gospels profess to record the historical events; the Acts of the Apostles to summarize the witness of both Peter and Paul, shared by the other apostles, first to the objective reality of these events and then to the faith to which they gave rise; the Epistles to elaborate the meaning of these events in the life of the church and its members; and the book of Revelation to deal with these same events in terms of their eternal and transcendental significance. That this is the attitude of the New Testament writers seems to me inescapable. But can we accept the claim that their faith had any adequate historical foundation? Is this credible in the twentieth century? What evidence can be adduced in its support?

## Christianity: its unique claims

Before we turn to consider the evidence as such we should, I think, pause to observe that the answer to this question will go a very long way towards providing the answer to our second major question about the Christian faith: whether it can justly be regarded as unique in its authority and final in its claims. For an examination of its historical origins will necessarily lead us to consider, in subsequent chapters, the evidence for three crucial tenets of Christian belief: first, that Jesus Christ was not merely a very good man who could point men to God more effectively than any other human teacher, but was himself God incarnate;

17

secondly, that the death he died cannot be explained simply as a tragedy of martyrdom, a supreme example of self-sacrifice, or even an enacted parable of divine love, but only as God's unique remedy for human sin; and thirdly, that he was in fact raised again on the third day, and that this resurrection must – in the light of the record of both his life and teaching – be regarded as a divine authentication both of the reality of his claims and the efficacy of his atoning death.

No-one in their senses would deny for a moment that the other world religions include much that is true and helpful, or that Christians can learn a great deal from the earnestness and devotion of their followers. In the Christian view, *all* that is true ultimately comes from God, mediated through Christ himself as the eternal 'Word' of the Father. But the other world religions also comprise much that is false and misleading – pre-eminently in the fact that they inevitably deny, at least by implication, God's unique revelation of himself in the incarnation, atonement and resurrection of Jesus. So the questions the Christian must inevitably ask himself are these. If God could have *adequately* revealed himself in any other way, would he have gone to the incredible length of the manger of Bethlehem and all that the incarnation involved? That, surely, would not make sense. Again, if God could have found *any* other solution to the problem of human sin, would he have gone all the way, in the person of his Son, to the cross of Calvary? That, too, would not make sense.

Precisely the same questions may be used to demonstrate that the Christian faith is not only unique but final. For if God has so revealed himself, what repetition or addition can be required or envisaged? And if God has in this way reconciled men to himself, what further remedy for sin can either God or man desire? Inevitably, therefore, the Christian faith claims for itself, in the words of Stephen Neill, that it is the 'only form of faith for men', and by its own claim to truth it inescapably 'casts the shadow of falsehood, or at least of imperfect truth, on every other system'. Here there is such a sharply contrasted thesis and antithesis that no synthesis or syncretism is possible. 'This Christian claim', he recognizes, is naturally offensive to the adherents of every other religious system. It is almost as offensive to modern man, brought up in the atmosphere of relativism, in which tolerance is regarded almost as the highest of the virtues. But we must not suppose that this claim to universal validity is something that can quietly be removed from the Gospel without changing it into something entirely different from what it is. The mission of Jesus was limited to the Jews and did not look immediately beyond them; but his life, his method and his message do not make sense, unless they are interpreted in the light of his own conviction that he was in fact the final and decisive word of God to men .... For the human sickness there is one specific remedy, and this is it. There is no other (Neill, *Christian Faith*, pp.16f.).

This is a stupendous assertion. Is it credible? And what standing has a lawyer, anyway, in such a study? Should it not rather be left to the historian and the theologian, as those professionally qualified to evaluate the historical evidence and then assess its significance? But it may be suggested in reply that in this case a significant part of the historical evidence comes from a consideration of facts and circumstances which must, from their very nature, be weighed and examined in a way which is not unfamiliar to the lawyer. He will necessarily be dependent on others for an evaluation of the documentary evidence as such; but he has, perhaps, a certain competence of his own in deciding what that evidence seems to establish, and must claim the right to assess the conclusions of the experts by his own criteria.

Now for all the details of the origins of Christianity we are dependent on the New Testament, to which we must soon turn our attention. But is there no documentary evidence whatever from non-Christian sources? Can no pagan or Jewish writers be cited in support?

## Extra-biblical evidence

### a. Roman

The answer is that such evidence does exist, but that it is understandably somewhat meagre. The earliest reference which has come down to us from any Roman document is in a letter written from Bithynia by the younger Pliny to the Emperor Trajan in about AD 110, in which he gives a picture of the early Christian community gathering in the early morning, once a week, to 'sing a hymn to Christ as to a god', and again, on the evening of the same day, to partake of a common meal. They refused to worship the imperial statue or the images of the gods, they lived exemplary lives, and some of them were willing to face death rather than deny their faith. There is also a terse reference in Tacitus, dated some five years later, to 'Christ, who was executed in the reign of Tiberius by the procurator Pontius Pilate' (*Annals* xi.44); and it is distinctly possible that, when he adds that 'A most mischievous superstition, thus checked for the moment, again broke out', he is bearing indirect and unconscious testimony to the conviction of the early church that the Christ who had been crucified had risen from the grave. There is also a probable reference to Christ in Suetonius, dated about AD 120, where he tells us that Claudius expelled the Jews from Rome because they were constantly making disturbances at the instigation of 'Chrestus' – for it seems that Suetonius mistook the split in the Jewish community in Rome which resulted from the Christian proclamation that Christ was still alive for a factional strife in which he was himself the leader of one of the parties (*Life of Claudius. Cf.* Dunkerley, pp.25f.).

### b. Secondary

In addition, there is a certain amount of secondary evidence, in the form of quotations from earlier pagan writers preserved in the books of third-century Christian authors. Origen, for example, states that Phlegon (a freedman of the Emperor Hadrian who was born about AD 80) mentioned that the founder of Christianity had made certain predictions which had proved true. Again, Julius Africanus informs us that 'Thallus, in the third book of his history' attributed the darkness at the crucifixion of Christ to an eclipse of the sun; and there is good reason to believe that this Thallus was a Samaritan historian who wrote about the middle of the first century (*cf.* Dunkerley, pp.27ff.). If this identification is correct, then from this and other evidence it seems clear that the circumstances surrounding the origin of Christianity were being discussed by non-Christians at a very early date. It is also distinctly possible that an inscription found in Nazareth in which the Emperor – either Claudius or possibly Tiberius – expressed his displeasure at reports he had heard of the removal of dead bodies from their graves, and even threatened the death penalty for such actions, represents an echo of the report which must surely have reached Rome about the crucifixion of one accused of political pretensions whose body had subsequently disappeared from the tomb (*cf.* Blaiklock, pp.28f.). But however that may be, the pagan evidence for the historicity of Jesus and his crucifixion under Pontius Pilate is such that it would be accepted without question in relation to anyone else.

*c. Jewish*

When we turn to Jewish sources the testimony of Josephus in his *Jewish War*, written between AD 70 and 75, is somewhat controversial. In the Greek version there are no references to Christ whatever, but there are some eight references in the Slavonic (or old Russian) version. These are often discounted, but it is at least possible that this version was based on a Greek translation of an earlier Aramaic draft which Josephus is known to have made. Be that as it may, his *Jewish Antiquities*, of some twenty years later, includes references to John the Baptist, to James 'the brother of Jesus, who was called Christ', and to Jesus himself in a longer passage which has been the subject of much controversy. Its essence reads as follows: 'And there arose about this time Jesus, a wise man, if indeed he should be called a man. For he was a doer of marvellous deeds, a teacher of men.... This man was the Christ. And when Pilate had condemned him to the cross at the instigation of our own leaders, those who had loved him from the first did not cease. For he appeared to them on the third day alive again . . . . and even now the tribe of Christians named after him is not extinct' (*Jewish Antiquities* xviii. 3.3).

This has often been dismissed as a Christian interpolation, on the grounds that it goes considerably further than would be likely from a non-Christian. But it would be equally plausible to argue that it does not go quite so far as might be expected from a Christian interpolation. Some of its phrases, of course, may well have been written in a vein of sarcasm, and it has even been described as a 'masterpiece of non-committal statement'. But whether or not it has been subjected to any Christian 'editing', it is difficult to ignore it completely, since it has as good manuscript evidence as anything in Josephus.

There are also a number of relevant references in the *Mishna*, or oral law (*i.e.* 'tradition of the elders', compiled between 100 BC and AD 200) and in the *Gemara* (*i.e.* comments of the Rabbis, compiled between AD 200 and 500). One of these begins, 'On the eve of Passover they hanged Yeshu of Nazareth.' Another reads, 'Rabbi Shimeon ben Azzai said . . . "such-an-one is a bastard of an adulteress"'; and a third, 'Rabbi Eliezer said 'Balaam looked forth and saw that there was a man, born of a woman, who should rise up and seek to make himself God, and to cause the whole world to go astray . . . and he will deceive and say that he departeth and cometh again at the end".'

These and other passages are accepted as references to Jesus by J. Klausner, a Jewish scholar, in his study *Jesus of Nazareth* (pp.27, 34f.). Naturally enough, they are of a hostile nature; but they are of considerable value as providing independent evidence, which can scarcely be called in question, not only to the historicity of Christ but to stories which were current about the unusual circumstances of his birth (with a scurrilous interpretation, which was, perhaps, only to be expected), his divine claims, his crucifixion and his reputed resurrection.

*d. Archaeological*

A brief reference must also be made to the testimony of archaeology. One of the most intriguing problems is posed by the Sator-Rotas acrostic, which takes the form of a complete word square (and perfect palindrome) and was regarded for centuries as having almost magical powers.[3] Its surface meaning – something to the effect that 'the sower holds the wheels of the plough with care' – could not possibly account for its widespread use in the early church. A persuasive conjecture about its secret meaning is that its letters, if arranged in the form of a cross, represent a twice-repeated 'Pater Noster' plus an additional A and 0 (standing for Alpha and Omega – or Jesus as the beginning and the end, the origin and the goal of all creation). As Dunkerley says, 'We may surmise that the original author in the first place arranged the two sacred words Pater Noster in the form of a cross, perhaps writing them on an actual cross of wood or even of papyrus, as a kind of holy remembrancer or aid to devotion. Then, at a time of persecution – perhaps the Neronian – he framed the square to contain yet conceal the beloved teaching. Lacking four letters, however, for a five-word square, he very skilfully chose the other two sacred letters, A and O ... and repeated them twice. The very fact ... of the difficulty ... of getting an exact and satisfactory interpretation of the sentence may itself point in this direction – he did his best within the limits of the available letters, but the result was not entirely perfect' (Dunkerley, p.61).

Read differently – and without any rearrangement whatever – the same acrostic can be seen as again including the sign of the cross formed by the repetition, vertically and horizontally, of the word 'Tenet' (he holds) – attention being called to this concealed cross by the T (an accepted

---

[3] If this suggestion is correct, the original symbol, in the form of a crucifix, would have read:

```
              [A]
               P
               A
               T
               E
               R
[A] P A T E R N O S T E R [O]
               O
               S
               T
               E
               R
              [O]
```

and the ultimate palindrome, in what was probably the older of the two forms in which it has been found:

| R | O | T | A | S |
|---|---|---|---|---|
| O | P | E | R | A |
| T | E | N | E | T |
| A | R | E | P | O |
| S | A | T | O | R |

symbol of the cross in the primitive church, according to the *Epistle of Barnabas* ix.8) with which both the vertical and horizontal bars begin and end. This would represent a vivid reminder not only of the centrality of the cross, with its message of forgiveness, but of the keeping power of the risen Lord which could, and did, sustain those going through the agonies of martyrdom. And this acrostic was in use very early indeed, since it has been found even in the ruins of Pompeii, destroyed in AD79 (*cf.* Dunkerley, p.58).

Another very common Christian symbol, from the earliest days, was the sign of a fish. The significance of this was that the five letters in the Greek word for fish (*ichthys*) stand for 'Jesus Christ, Son of God, Saviour' – which represents a brief, but remarkably comprehensive, Christian creed.

None of this, of course, adds very much to what we already know from the pages of the New Testament. What these archaeological discoveries prove is that there is testimony, even outside the New Testament, to what Christians believed at an exceedingly early date. And archaeological excavations have again and again vindicated the historical accuracy of the New Testament documents – *e.g.* the Acts of the Apostles – in regard to details which had previously been called in question, or even ridiculed, by critics.

## The New Testament evidence

When we turn to the New Testament we find an abundance of detail which is in marked contrast to the paucity of non-Christian material. Nor is this in any way surprising. On the contrary, it is precisely what we might expect. Neither Josephus nor Tacitus lived in Palestine at the time when Jesus of Nazareth lived and taught, or when he died on a Roman gibbet; and nothing has come down to us written by any non-Christian Jew, Roman or Greek who had any first-hand evidence to record. Roman historians and men of letters were scarcely likely to have taken much interest in 'an obscure peasant teacher in an unimportant frontier province', so it would not have been surprising if the humble birth of Christianity had gone completely unnoticed in such circles; and it has been remarked that since Josephus wrote with the intention of re-establishing

Judaism with Roman society in general and the imperial house in particular, he naturally kept to a minimum any material which would irritate Roman readers.[4] It is clear from the Gospels, moreover, that Jesus himself led no rebellion and made no such dramatic gesture in defiance of authority as would attract the attention of a Roman historian. Instead, he confided the testimony to who he was, what he had done and what he had taught to a little band of chosen eyewitnesses, feeble as they were, and to the work which the divine Spirit was to do in them and through them.

We must, therefore, take as our major starting-point the faith and teaching of the primitive church as we find it throughout the New Testament, for about this there can be no doubt whatever. The early Christians clearly believed – and we shall discuss these phrases later – that Jesus of Nazareth was the Son of God, the very agent of creation, who had been made man, had proclaimed the kingdom of God, wrought miracles, gone about doing good, and had finally died on the cross for the sins of mankind. But on the third day he rose again, showed himself alive to his disciples by 'many infallible proofs' and ascended into heaven, with the promise that one day he would return to usher in a new heaven and new earth, with the resurrection of the dead and the final judgment. So they proceeded to apply to him all manner of honorific titles. They called him 'Messiah, Son of Man, Son of David, Son of God, Redeemer, Saviour, Kyrios, Lord, Logos, God' (Zahrnt, p.137). And the fact that Paul included the Aramaic prayer '*Marana-tha*' ('Come, O Lord') in a letter to a Greek-speaking community (1 Corinthians 16:22) 'leads us to the conclusion that Jesus was not exalted to the position of "Lord" in Antioch, when Christianity moved into the Hellenistic world and came under the influence of certain ideas of Greek religion; he must have been called upon and revered as the exalted Lord even in the primitive Aramaic-speaking community' (Zahrnt, pp.127f.)

---

[4]*Cf.* Michael Green, *World on the run*, p.33. This book gives an excellent summary of the historical evidence.

## The biblical Christ and the historical Jesus

But the question necessarily arises as to whether this teaching about the exalted Christ has any vital connection with the historical Jesus on whom it was professedly based. For many years it has been fashionable to postulate a veritable gulf between the 'Lord of faith' and the 'Jesus of history' (Moule, *Phenomenon*, pp.44f.). At first the emphasis was firmly placed on an attempt to get behind 'Pauline Christianity' and to rediscover the Jesus who walked and talked beside the Sea of Galilee. The attitude of mind of the scholars of what may be termed the era of Liberal Protestantism was that the Jesus of history meant something very different from the Jesus preached by the church.

> It meant Jesus as we can know him when we have dismantled the Church's preaching about him, and have penetrated behind it to find the real, actual, historical Jesus, Jesus as he historically was, Jesus the human historical personality, unsullied by dogma and undistorted by later ecclesiastical interpretation, be it Pauline or Johannine, Jewish or Greek.... The Liberal Protestant scholars believed that when this process of piercing through the creeds, of dismantling dogmatic accretions upon the original Jesus, was complete, they would be presented with a recognisable, reliable portrait of the real Jesus, and were confident that he could form a permanent basis for a reconstructed version of Christianity. They were fond of contrasting the religion *about* Jesus, which they viewed with suspicion, with the religion *of* Jesus, which was the true basis and origin of Christianity (R.P.C. Hanson, p.29).

Today this quest for the 'Jesus of history' has largely been abandoned as a failure. This is partly because of the attitude of mind which underlay the quest, and partly because of the nature of the Gospel records. The older Liberal theologians began with an *a priori* rejection of everything miraculous; so they believed they could reconstruct a historical Jesus by discarding all the supernatural elements in the Gospels. But this attempt was doomed to failure, for they found that the miracles were so intertwined with the teaching, and the supernatural with the natural, that they could not discard the one and retain the other (*cf.* Schaeffer, p.52).

The Gospels on their part, moreover, were never intended to provide the material for a biography of Jesus. They do not attempt to give a 'Life of Jesus' as such, but to proclaim his words and actions as God's revelation and salvation in word and deed. They are basically a proclamation of good news: good news about one whom the writers had come to believe in as God's final self-revelation to man. They cannot – and do not – claim to be dispassionate historical records written in a spirit of purely objective enquiry, or indeed to be more than very fragmentary records at that (John 20:30f.; 21:25).

More recently, therefore, the tendency has been to put the emphasis almost exclusively on the Lord of faith rather than the Jesus of history. Rudolf Bultmann, for example, has maintained that the historical enquirer can be sure of little more about the latter than that 'a man called Jesus of Nazareth really lived' and that the church, which lives by faith in the exalted Christ, needs to know 'no more than this basic fact, that Jesus was a person belonging to history and hence more than a mere symbol or mythical figure'. For true faith, as Otto Betz puts it,

> will not rest on scientifically established, universally acceptable facts. It clings to the Word of God, which is outside human control. It is this Word alone, proclaimed by the New Testament Church, which leads us to the crucified and risen Lord. The statement that Jesus of Nazareth is the Christ, the Saviour of mankind, cannot be demonstrated as a general and inevitable truth. It only becomes true in the venture of faith, the venture of a free, personal decision (Betz, pp.12f.).

## History confirmed by experience

But on that basis we should be faced with only two alternatives. We should either have to choose the existentialist road, preach the 'Christ event', and challenge our fellow-men to make an act of faith in Christ virtually regardless of any historical foundation; or we should have to accept the church's interpretation of Jesus as authoritative, and leave it at that. But the church has never had the right to delineate its own picture of Christ and then demand our unquestioning assent to every detail. 'On the contrary', as R.P.C Hanson says,

the Church from the earliest period has produced historical evidence to support its claim without ever maintaining that historical evidence alone was enough.... We must therefore conclude *neither* that Christian belief is totally emancipated from a consideration of historical evidence, *nor* that the truth of Christianity rests, or can be made to rest, on historical evidence alone (*Vindications*, p.67).

In other words, Christian faith can never dispense with the historical facts to which it owes its origin and to which we must continually return, but those facts themselves stand in need of the elucidation and application with which they were always accompanied in the preaching and teaching of the apostolic church.

## A greatly exaggerated gap

The fact is that both those who followed the quest for the Jesus of history (as distinct from the Christ of the apostolic proclamation) and those who concentrate today almost exclusively on the Lord of faith are postulating far too wide and unbridgeable a gulf between the two. The more extreme exponents of what is known as Form Criticism have gone so far as to maintain that the material in the Gospels has been so moulded and adapted by the primitive church that no purely historical figure can be identified; but more recently some of the disciples of Bultmann have themselves recognized that they are in danger, at this point, of 'losing themselves in a world of myth and make-believe'. We must always remember, and insist, that the preaching and teaching of the apostolic church must have been firmly based on a real, historical person who had actually – and very recently

– lived a life and given teaching of the unique quality to which the preaching of the apostles called men. Clearly it is true, as J. G. Herder pointed out, long before the age of Form Criticism, that 'Christianity did not begin with the writing of gospels'. Primarily it began with the proclamation of the life, death and resurrection of Jesus, and also with 'exegesis, teaching, consolation, admonition, *preaching* . . . including the rehearsal of narratives, parables and sayings' (*cf.* Zahrnt, pp.95ff.).

But Geza Vermes, a Jewish scholar with a keen interest in Gospel criticism, has expressed his profound scepticism about any suggestion 'that the composition of the Gospels is due entirely to the didactic-theological requirements of the primitive Church, and that they were never in any way intended to be "historical"'. For if the Evangelists 'were primarily resolved to teach Christian doctrine,' he argues,

> was it not rather inept to adopt a biographical literary style, which provides liveliness and colour but at the expense of simplicity and clarity? Their story of Jesus is replete with Palestinian ideas, customs, linguistic peculiarities and *realia* of all sorts, incomprehensible to non-Jewish readers and demanding continuous interpretative digressions which were bound to be catechetically harmful. . . . Early teachers such as Paul, James, the author of Didache, found in any case no advantage in 'biography' for the transmission of theological expositions, moral exhortations, and disciplinary or liturgical rules, and opted sensibly for a direct method of communication. It is therefore difficult to avoid concluding that the evangelists chose to tell the life of Jesus because, whatever else they may have aimed at, they were determined to recount history, however unprofessionally. And if they include circumstances which were doctrinally embarrassing, it is because they genuinely form part of the narrative. In that case, Bultmann's famous dictum to the effect that nothing can be known of Jesus' story or personality 'because the early Christian sources show no interest in either' (*Jesus and the Word*, p.14), becomes a plain misjudgment (Vermes, pp.55f.).

Clearly, then, we must reject any idea that the Gospels were not intended by the Evangelists to be accepted as honest accounts of what Jesus actually taught and said; but we must also realize that they were concerned with testimonies of faith, rather than cold historiography. As a result Bornkamm can insist:

> The Gospels justify neither resignation nor scepticism. Rather they bring before our eyes, in very different fashion from what is customary in chronicles and presentations of history, the historical person of Jesus with the utmost vividness. Quite clearly what the Gospels report concerning the message, the deeds and the history of Jesus is still distinguished by an authenticity, a freshness and a distinctiveness not in any way effaced by the Church's Easter Faith. These features point us directly to the earthly figure of Jesus (Bornkamm, p.24).

This quotation is particularly striking as coming from one of Bultmann's own disciples; and it should be seen, I think, against the background of the detailed evidence provided by Moule in *The Phenomenon of the New Testament* that, although the Evangelists clearly wrote their Gospels in the light of their faith in the resurrection, they took great care *not* to depict the Jesus of the Gospels in the terms used in the Epistles of the glorified Lord (*cf*.p.31, below).

It is vitally important, therefore, to hold two seemingly opposite, yet complementary, facts in juxtaposition. First, that there is a very real sense in which we can today know the earthly Jesus only through the proclamation of the apostolic church, for it is solely on the testimony of the disciples that we can hear his voice and see him as he was. Secondly, it is going much too far to state that 'Everything that Jesus said and did, everything that happened earlier, the earthly life of Jesus, is completely bathed in the glow of the Easter event. The understanding of the history of Jesus in the Gospels is governed by the resurrection to such an extent that the boundaries between his actions before Easter and his actions after Easter are blurred' (*cf.* Zahrnt, p.78). For although the Evangelists themselves, it is true, must have viewed the whole history of Jesus in the light of Easter, it remains true that 'they nevertheless put the proclamation of Christ within the framework of the earthly life of Jesus' (Zahrnt, p.100). Thus C. F. D. Moule has shown how carefully Luke 'does not attribute to the participants in his story of the ministry of Jesus the same explicit estimate of Jesus as he attributes to the apostles when they are speaking of the risen Jesus. That is to say, he represents the contemporaries of Jesus in his earthly life as speaking of him with reserve. They do not use the great Christological titles of the post-resurrection preaching. Yet, equally, Luke leaves not a shadow of doubt that the one to whom the exalted titles of the Church's proclamation are applied is the same man, Jesus of Nazareth, about whom he tells his story in his Gospel' (Moule, *Phenomenon*, p.57).

What is beyond dispute is that every attempt to date the Gospels late in the first century has now definitely failed, crushed under the weight of convincing evidence. If the majority of five hundred witnesses to the resurrection were still alive around AD 55 (see below), then our Gospels must have begun to appear when many who had seen and heard the earthly Jesus – including some of the apostles – were still available to confirm or question the traditions. Not only so, but the Evangelists, as Otto Betz observes, stood in a double relationship to Christ – both horizontal and vertical:

On the one hand through the current of tradition, which carried the words and acts of the earthly Jesus to them; on the other through faith in the heavenly Christ, present in the preached word, in the Holy Spirit and in the sacraments. The modern distinction between Jesus as a historical figure and Christ as a historical force did not exist for them (Betz, p.11).

## Some examples of the apostolic proclamation

### a. The resurrection

Now the attitude of the apostolic church and the content of the apostolic confession can be readily ascertained from documents of indisputable authority. I have already referred to the fact that no competent scholar today questions the Pauline authorship of 1 Corinthians. It is a matter of general consensus, too, that it was written between AD 52 and 57 (with 55, perhaps, as the most probable date). But the apostle tells us, in 1 Corinthians 15:3, first that he had already given the Corinthians an account by word of mouth of what he was now committing to paper (which would take the date back to AD 49, or very soon after), and then that he had himself received the tradition he was about to record from those who were apostles before him. This certainly takes us back to his visit to Jerusalem, about which he gives such a solemn assurance in Galatians 1:18–20, when he had stayed for fifteen days with Peter, but 'saw none of the other apostles – only James, the Lord's brother'.

About this visit C. H. Dodd has insisted that it took place 'almost certainly not more than seven years, possibly no more than four' after Jesus was crucified (*Founder*, p.168); and it is significant that in 1 Corinthians 15:5 and 7 Paul specifically cites both Peter and James as independent witnesses to having seen the risen Lord. It is probable, moreover, that Paul had in fact received the substance of this tradition, from Ananias and the Christian community in Damascus, *immediately* after his own conversion. And in 1 Corinthians 15:11 he insists that this was no private proclamation of his own, but the common testimony of all the apostles – based, from the very first, on what the eyewitnesses themselves had recounted.

Something had happened to these men, which they could describe only by saying that they had 'seen the Lord'. This is not an appeal to any generalized 'Christian experience'. It refers to a particular series of occurrences, unique in character, unrepeatable, and confined to a limited period (Dodd, *Founder*, p.168).

The substance of the relevant tradition is the terse statement, the very structure and wording of which suggest a credal formula, that 'Christ died for our sins according to the Scriptures, that he was buried, that he was raised on the third day according to the Scriptures' (1 Corinthians 15:3f.). But it is significant that this is immediately supported by the unequivocal assertion that the risen Christ was not only seen by Peter, the twelve, James and the other apostles, but, on one occasion, by more than five hundred Christians at once, the majority of whom were still alive when this letter was written. So this is a piece of historical evidence of outstanding importance. We know who wrote it, approximately when he wrote it, and the way in which he gratuitously exposed himself to contradiction and criticism if what he wrote was not in accordance with the testimony of the many eyewitnesses who were still alive.

## b. The relation between Jesus and God

It is also significant that in this same Epistle we have a verse which echoes the teaching of the prologue to John's Gospel. In the context of a discussion about food offered to idols the apostle states that 'for us there is but one God, the Father, from whom all things came and for whom we live; and there is but one Lord, Jesus Christ, through whom all things came and through whom we live' (1 Corinthians 8:6). This is closely in tune with John's affirmation that 'In the beginning was the Word, and the Word was with God, and the Word was God. He was with God in the beginning. Through him all things were made; without him nothing was made that has been made' (John 1:1–3; *cf*. Colossians 1:16 and Hebrews 1:10) – except that Paul makes no explicit distinction between the pre-incarnate 'Word' and the incarnate Christ. And in the Epistle to the Romans – again accepted by all scholars as indisputably Pauline – the apostle summarizes the gospel he had been commissioned to preach by stating that the Jesus of history, 'a descendant of David by human genealogy' (Romans 1:3, JBP), had been declared to be the Son of God 'by a mighty act in that he rose from the dead' (Romans 1:4, NEB). This is the very sum and substance of the preaching of the apostles as we find this recorded in the Acts and their teaching as we find it set forth in the Epistles.

## c. References to the life and teaching of Jesus

Even if we confine ourselves to those Epistles which are indubitably Pauline, there are many passing references to the facts recorded in the Gospels. It is clear that to Paul

Jesus was a real man, 'born of a woman, born under the law' (Galatians 4:4) – and, as we have seen, of Davidic stock (Romans 1:3). His 'meekness and gentleness' (2 Corinthians 10:1) were known and admired, yet he was 'betrayed' (1 Corinthians 11:23) and crucified by the rulers of this world (1 Corinthians 2:8), the Jews themselves being basically responsible (1 Thessalonians 2:14–15). The Last Supper is recounted at some length (1 Corinthians 11:23–25). There are also echoes of the teaching of Jesus – *e.g.* in the apostle's emphasis on love as fulfilling the law (Romans 13:10; Galatians 5:14), and on paying tribute to those to whom it is due (Romans 13:7; Mark 12:6–7). In regard to marriage, moreover, the apostle carefully distinguishes between the commandment of the Lord and his own judgment (1 Corinthians 7:10–12, 25). It has been justly remarked that

> The charge against Paul of being 'the great innovator' (or the great corrupter) of the Gospel must be dropped for good and all . . . . Original Paul was, but the thing about which he wrote with such individual and creative power was not his own discovery or invention. It was the common tradition of the Christian faith which he took over from those who were 'in Christ' before him. Is not this a conclusion of quite capital importance? (Hunter, p.150).

The Petrine authorship of 1 Peter has been much debated, the chief argument to the contrary being the quality of the Greek. But it would seem very possible that it was in fact Silvanus (probably to be identified with the Silas of Acts 15 and 16, and a New Testament 'prophet' in his own right) who was its actual penman; and there are excellent grounds for believing that the apostle Peter was its real author (Selwyn, pp.7–17). The letter certainly includes a number of natural, unselfconscious touches which seem to indicate the testimony of an eyewitness and would be particularly appropriate to Peter. It refers to the sinlessness of Christ (1 Peter 2:22), his role as Shepherd of his people (2:25; 5:4); his patience and forbearance at his trial (2:23), his sufferings (1:11), his atoning death (2:24) and his promised glory (1:11). It is also significant that the meaning of the crucifixion is explained by reference to precisely the same chapter in the Old Testament as that to which Luke tells us that Jesus himself referred on the way to the garden of Geth-semane (2:24f.; *cf.* Luke 22:37). As for the author of 1 John, he bases his whole message on 'that...which we have heard, which we have seen with our own eyes, which we looked upon and touched with our own hands' (changing abruptly, in these last two phrases, to the aorist of a historical event) – for the Word of life, he says, was actually 'made visible; we have seen it and bear our testimony' (1 John 1:1f., NEB).

## The reliability of the apostolic witness

So much for the Epistles. Even this lightning survey serves not only to substantiate the summary of the teaching of the primitive church with which our consideration of the testimony of the New Testament began, but also to show that this teaching included much of the material recorded in the Gospels. Surely, then, we have a right to ask, with C. F. D. Moule, whether these apostolic confessions were justified, whether they were based on any adequate foundation, and what can be reconstructed by deductions from them. And he tells us that the answers to these questions seem, in certain quarters, to be beginning to be:

Yes, the apostolic confessions are justified, because the figure which emerges from the most radically critical attempt at reconstruction is the figure of one whose teaching and message were of the very same quality as attaches to the figure of the apostolic proclamation. The Jesus retrieved by the most careful criticism (and it is, I think, perverse to assert that such critical reconstruction can accomplish nothing) is no longer the rationally acceptable moralist of the Liberal Protestants, but a 'catalyst' – a person whose very presence precipitates a crisis of faith and forces 'existential' decision (Moule, *Phenomenon*, pp.45ff.).

D. E. Nineham, too, whose attachment to a somewhat extreme variety of Form Criticism is well known, summarizes the position, as he views it, when he writes:

As we have seen, it is possible to some extent to reconstruct the units of tradition on which the Gospels are
based. When we do reconstruct them, not only do we
find that the units on which St Mark is based presuppose
*broadly* the same Christ as the finished Gospel, but we
find that other units, preserved independently in other
places and used by the other evangelists, also preserve a
fundamentally similar figure. Our basic picture of Christ
is thus carried back to a point only a quarter of a century
or so after his death; and when we bear in mind the
wonderfully retentive memory of the Oriental, who,
being unable to read and write, had perforce to cultivate
accuracy of memory, it will not seem surprising that we
can often be virtually sure that what the tradition is
offering us are the authentic deeds, and especially the
authentic words, of the historic Jesus (Nineham, pp.50f.).

Nor is this any mere generalization. On the contrary, A. M.
Ramsey, Betz, Moule and other scholars refer to point after
point in the Gospel records which stand up, in their view,
to the most radical criticism. Betz, for example, mentions
*inter alia* the parables, the proclamation of the kingdom,
the teaching about the sabbath, the disputes with the
Pharisees and Sadducees, the miracles and the Messianic
consciousness and confession of the Jesus of the Synoptic
Gospels (Betz, pp.48ff., 3ff., 78ff., 58ff., and 83ff., respectively). Similarly, Moule reminds us that 'what the
apostles remembered of Jesus' ministry included his own
interpretation of it, however much and however often this
had, at the time, been misunderstood. In a sense, the
post-Easter *interpretation* was only a *rediscovery* of what
had been there in the teaching of Jesus himself' (*Phenomenon*, p.46 – citing O. Cullmann). Moule also emphasizes
that there are many passages in the Gospels in which an
authentic picture of Jesus

would seem to have fairly forced its way through an
atmosphere still alien to it . . . Jesus, who was not afraid
of earning the reputation of being a gluttonous man and
a wine-bibber, a friend of tax-collectors and sinners,
emerges in the Gospel traditions as one who risked

obloquy also for consorting with disreputable women; and the extraordinary thing is that writers who must themselves have hated and feared the very risks they are describing and who were themselves not wholly free from a repressive attitude, yet, despite themselves, succeed in presenting a strangely convincing picture of Jesus...The simplicity and surefootedness of the delineation are amazing (*Phenomenon*, p.65).

He mentions a number of other features in the tradition, too, which were faithfully recorded in spite of a tendency in its transmitters which would militate against them. Examples of such features are Jesus' challenge to Israel to fulfil her destiny; the retention of the Semitic 'Amen' to introduce (rather than conclude) some of his statements, in a way without parallel in rabbinic usage, because (as Käsemann puts it) 'in his person and words the Kingdom of God manifested is presence and authority'; his identification of John the Baptist with Elijah, with all which that implied; and his association of baptism with teaching about death and resurrection (*Phenomenon*, pp.63–73). All this, he says, gives the lie, on the one hand, 'to the notion that the Church's estimate of Jesus is something which Christians unconsciously adopted in the course of time, and then simply assumed as having obtained from the beginning'. Similarly, certain aspects of Jesus' attitude and ministry which have survived in the traditions, 'despite the fact that the early Christians do not seem to have paid particular attention to them or to have recognized their Christological significance', bear 'witness in a subtle and paradoxical way to the identity of the Jesus of the ministry with the Lord who was worshipped, and to the tenacity and continuity of the traditions about him' (*Phenomenon*, pp.75f.).

The conclusion that the primitive church did not exercise anything approaching the creative influence over the material we find in the Gospels as is postulated by the more extreme Form Critics is reinforced by the sharp divisions between them on point after point in their attempted reconstructions. Their method strike the lawyer as basically more subjective than objective, for every scholar seems to make a different selection of so-called facts, and then dub the rest fancy. 'The inevitable result', as R. P. C. Hanson says, 'is that all the facts might as well be fancy because, while it is agreed that *some* of them are almost certainly facts, nobody can produce any satisfactory reason why this selection should be regarded as facts and not fancy, rather than that one, or that one, or that one. It is not merely that every critic plays the game differently from the others, but that every critic makes his own rules' (*Vindications*, p.30).

It is interesting in this context to see how a classical scholar such as A. N. Sherwin-White regards the scepticism of many New Testament critics, and how strange he finds their attitude when compared with that of those scholars who examine the history of a variety of classical figures whose acts and words are considerably less well-documented. And his own examination of the New Testament material in the light of Roman law and customs is, I think, of considerable significance (Sherwin-White, *passim*).

For myself, then, I stand unhesitatingly with C. F. D. Moule when he says that 'the alternatives are not either mere history coupled with a rationalistic estimate of Jesus as a very good man (an estimate such as could be made by an atheist), or commitment to a preached but unauthenticated Lord . . . . The creed is not a series of assertions made in a vacuum, but a summary of value-judgments reached on the basis of eye-witness testimony to an event' (*Phenomenon*, p.79). Put somewhat differently, we must agree with Otto Betz that to accept Jesus' Messianic claim – with all that this involves – is an act of faith.

> But it is not conjured up out of nothing; it is based on history. It is the 'yes' of faith to the claim of a historical personage. Apart from such an assent there is only the decisive 'no' which is a denial of Jesus' messianic claim. It is the 'no' of Caiaphas and the Jews in Jerusalem. There is no third possibility. For whoever sees in Jesus the wandering rabbi, the proclaimer of the end of the world or the witness of faith, falls short of his own claim and the testimony of his disciples (Betz, p.114).

## How Jesus himself authenticates the Gospels

But not only do the Gospels bear their testimony to the unique figure which dominates their pages – which will, in large part, be the subject of the next chapter – but the unique figure himself may be said to authenticate the Gospels. It was John Stuart Mill who said:

> It is of no use to say that Christ, as exhibited in the Gospels, is not historical, and that we know not how much of what is admirable has been super-added by the tradition of his followers. Who among his disciples or among their proselytes was capable of inventing the sayings of Jesus or of imagining the life and character revealed in the Gospels? Certainly not the fishermen of Galilee; as certainly not St Paul, whose character and idiosyncrasies were of a totally different sort; still less the early Christian writers, in whom nothing is more evident than that the good which was in them was all derived, as they always professed that it was derived, from the higher source (Mill, pp.253 f.).

Nor is this argument weakened by the fact that the writers of the Gospels relied, to a considerable extent, on oral tradition and written records (including, of course, the interdependence, in part, of the Synoptic Gospels). The more complex the strata of their sources, the greater the problem of the portrait they paint (*cf*. W. H. Griffith Thomas, p.71). As Rousseau justly remarked: 'It is more inconceivable that several men should have united to forge the Gospel than that a single person should have furnished the subject of it. The Gospel has marks of truth so great, so striking, so perfectly inimitable, that the inventor of it would be more astonishing than the hero' (*cf*. W. Robertson Nicoll, p.41).

## The apocryphal Gospels

The force of this argument is immensely increased when we compare the four canonical Gospels – all of which were almost certainly composed, in their present form, between

AD 65 and the end of the first century, at the latest – with the apocryphal Gospels of a century later. 'All who read them with any attention', says B. Harris Cowper in the preface to his translation, 'will see that they are fictions, and not histories, not traditions even, so much as legends'; and he adds: 'Before I undertook this work I never realised so completely as I do now the impassable character of the gulf which separates the genuine Gospels from these.'

It is interesting to compare this statement with the testimony of two men who have recently translated the canonical Gospels into colloquial English. 'I have read, in Greek and Latin, scores of myths,' writes J. B. Phillips, 'but I did not find the slightest flavour of myth here . . . . One sensed again and again that understatement which we have been taught to think is more "British" than Oriental. There is an almost childlike candour and simplicity . . . . No man could ever have invented such a character as Jesus. No man could have set down such artless and vulnerable accounts as these unless some real Event lay behind them.' And Phillips recounts that E. V. Rieu, a leading classical scholar who undertook the task of translating the Gospels because he had 'an intense desire to satisfy himself about their authenticity', testified that he found the whole material extraordinarily alive. 'It changed me', he said. 'My work changed me. And I came to the conclusion that these words bear the seal of the Son of Man and God' (Phillips, p.58; *cf.* Blaiklock, p.44).

## My own stance in this book

In the following chapters I shall base my conclusions about the person of Christ, the meaning of his death and the historicity of his resurrection on the New Testament as a whole, without more than a few passing references to whether the relevant evidence is derived from the Synoptic Gospels, the Fourth Gospel, those Epistles which are indubitably Pauline, or elsewhere. Professor Moule has argued persuasively 'that all four Gospels alike are to be interpreted as more than anything else evangelistic and apologetic in purpose; and that the Synoptic Gospels represent primarily the recognition that a vital element in evangelism is the plain story of what happened in the ministry of Jesus' (*Phenomenon*, p.113). The Fourth Gospel clearly includes a much more extensive interpretative element; but recent studies have shown how primitive and Palestinian is its background – and who are we to interpret the life and teachings of Jesus compared with the 'beloved disciple', to whom the record (if not the Gospel in its final form) in my belief assuredly goes back? (*Cf.* Temple, pp. x and xvi.)

As for the apostolic testimony, we have discussed the authority and exceedingly early date of some of the Epistles, and the remaining books of the New Testament do not differ from these at all significantly in their teaching. It is a strangely perverse attitude, as C. F. D. Moule has remarked, 'which, while quite unwarrantably hospitable to the latest irresponsible speculation by journalistic charlatans, insists on treating such serious documents as those which comprise the New Testament as though they had long ago been discredited' (*Phenomenon*, p.2).

But there is another vital factor in all this – the claim of the Bible to divine inspiration. We shall see in the next chapter that there can be no doubt – unless we are to make complete nonsense of the Gospels – that Christ himself paid repeated testimony to the divine authority of the Old Testament scriptures. Obviously, he could make no such comments about the New Testament documents, which had not yet been written; but he told his disciples that it was positively 'expedient' for them – impossible though this must have seemed – that he should leave them, because only so could they know the presence and power of the Holy Spirit in a new way. And he explicitly stated that among the benefits this experience would bring them would be that the Spirit would teach them all things and bring to their remembrance all that he had said to them (John 14:26), guide them into all truth and show them things about him which he himself could not teach them then (John 16:12–13). And if any men were ever possessed by the Spirit, it was the apostles and their immediate followers who gave us the New Testament. So I believe that these promises were fulfilled, and that these documents are not the unaided recollections of the disciples, but constitute a divinely authoritative record. But I shall not, of course, take this for granted in my argument; instead, I shall attempt to let the New Testament speak for itself.

The substance of this chapter can, I think, be summed up in the words of Bishop Stephen Neill:

> The Jesus Christ whom the Christian meets when he comes to the Holy Communion, who is made present to him in the proclamation of the Gospel in Christian worship, to whom he speaks when he prays, who speaks to him through the Holy Spirit, is the same Jesus who was born at a specific time and place in history, who lived a human life, who spoke certain words, did certain deeds, and suffered certain things, of which we have clear though far from complete knowledge' (in Zahrnt, p.6).

It is this which puts such a gulf between Christianity and those mystery religions with which it has sometimes been compared.

# 2
# The central figure: how are we to regard him?

Our study of the historical basis of Christianity has led us inexorably to the central figure that dominates the whole New Testament. To an extent unequalled in any other religion, the Christian faith rests four-square on the person of its founder, for it is profoundly true that 'Christianity is Christ' (Griffith Thomas).

The essence of Confucianism and Buddhism is the teachings and principles inculcated by Confucius and the Buddha respectively, not Confucius or the Buddha themselves, nor the facts about their lives or deaths. Even in Islam the towering figure of Muhammad owes its importance primarily to the fact that he is believed to have been the channel of divine revelation. It is the very words of God, as communicated to Muhammad by the archangel Gabriel and subsequently recorded in the Qur'ān, together with the further teaching provided by the stories which allegedly record the inspired Sunna or practice of the Prophet, that constitute the heart of the faith. A devout Muslim will always point to the Book and the Traditions, rather than to Muhammad himself, as God's supreme revelation.

In Christianity, on the other hand, the opposite is the case. The New Testament is, indeed, indispensable as our only authoritative source of information about the life, mission, death and resurrection of Jesus; but it is Jesus Christ himself, not the Bible, that constitutes the supreme revelation of God. Paul and the other New Testament writers are rightly regarded as messengers who declared and recorded the divine message; but Jesus was much more than even the supreme messenger, for he was himself the Message. To the Christian the written word of God, the Bible, always points to the living Word of the Father. The testimony of the apostles was that

> It was there from the beginning; we have heard it; we have seen it with our own eyes; we looked upon it, and felt it with our own hands; and it is of this we tell. Our theme is the word of life. This life was made visible; we have seen it and bear our testimony; we here declare to you the eternal life which dwelt with the Father and was made visible to us (1 John 1:1ff., NEB).

So we must now concentrate on Jesus Christ, and try to decide what answer we ourselves feel compelled to give to the most important question that has ever been asked: 'What do *you* think of the Christ?' (Matthew 22:42, RSV).

## Some miscellaneous opinions

He has certainly made an enormous impact on a wide variety of men and women all down the ages. The most radical and outspoken critics, among a motley of others, have paid notable tributes. Goethe, for example, wrote that 'I esteem the Gospels to be thoroughly genuine, for there shines forth from them the reflected splendour of a sublimity, proceeding from the person of Jesus Christ, and of as Divine a kind as was ever manifested upon earth'.[1] Strauss, for all his scepticism, conceded that 'With reference to all that bears upon the love of God and of our neighbour, upon purity of heart and upon the individual

[1] J. W. von Goethe, *Conversations with Eckerman* iii, p.371 (conveniently quoted in Ballard, p.251).

life, nothing can be added to the moral intuition which Jesus Christ has left us'.[2] Renan's view was that 'Jesus is in every respect unique, and nothing can be compared with him. Be the unlooked for phenomena of the future what they may, Jesus will not be surpassed'.[3] 'Can the Person whose history the Gospels relate be himself a man?' asked Rousseau. 'What sweetness, what purity in his manners! What affecting goodness in his instructions! What sublimity in his maxims! . . . . Yes, if the life and death of Socrates are those of a philosopher, the life and death of Jesus Christ are those of a God'.[4] And W. E. H. Lecky, in his *History of European Morals,* has written:

I have reserved for Christianity to present to the world an ideal character, which through all the changes of eighteen centuries has inspired the hearts of men with an impassioned love; has shown itself capable of acting on all ages, nations, temperaments, and conditions; has been not only the highest pattern of virtue but the strongest incentive to its practice; and has exercised so deep an influence that it may truly be said that the simple record of three short years of active life has done more to regenerate and to soften mankind than all the disquisitions of philosophers, and all the exhortations of moralists (Lecky, Vol. 11, p.88).

In his Bampton Lectures of 1866, Liddon records that Napoleon, conversing with Count Montholon on the rock of St Helena about the great figures of the ancient world and his own place among them, said:

Alexander, Caesar, Charlemagne, and I myself have founded great empires; but upon what did these creations of our genius depend? Upon force. Jesus alone founded his empire upon love, and to this very day millions would die for Him . . . . I think I understand something of human nature; and I tell you, all these were men, and I am a man: none else is like Him; Jesus Christ

[2]D. F. Strauss, *Life of Jesus* (People's edition), pp.625ff. (conveniently quoted in Ballard, pp.221f.).

[3]J. E. Renan, *Étude d'histoire religeuse,* p.175 (conveniently quoted in Ballard, p.251).

[4]Jean-Jacques Rousseau, *Émile* IV, ii, p.110 (conveniently quoted in Ballard, p.251).

was more than man .... I have inspired multitudes with such an enthusiastic devotion that they would have died for me, ... but to do this it was necessary that I should be *visibly* present with the electric influence of my looks, of my words, of my voice .... Christ alone has succeeded in so raising the mind of man to the Unseen, that it becomes insensible to the barriers of time and space. Across a chasm of eighteen hundred years, Jesus Christ makes a demand which is beyond all others difficult to satisfy .... He asks for the human heart; He will have it entirely to Himself. He demands it unconditionally; and forthwith His demand is granted. Wonderful! In defiance of time and space, the soul of man, with all its powers and faculties, becomes an annexation to the empire of Christ .... This phenomenon is unaccountable; it is altogether beyond the scope of man's creative powers. Time, the great destroyer, is powerless to extinguish this sacred flame; time can neither exhaust its strength nor put a limit to its range. This is it which strikes me most; I have often thought of it. This it is which proves to me quite convincingly the Divinity of Jesus Christ (Liddon, p.150).

Another, much shorter, tribute can be found in Hazlitt's Essay 'Of Persons one would wish to have seen'. This is a record of an informal discussion in a distinguished literary circle whose members are usually identified only by letters of the alphabet. Towards the end Charles Lamb, it seems, suggested Judas Iscariot and, when asked to justify this suggestion, said: 'I would fain see the face of him, who, having dipped his hand in the same dish as the Son of Man, could afterwards betray him. I have no conception of such a thing; nor have I ever seen any picture (not even Leonardo's very fine one) that gave me the least idea of it.' 'There is only one other person I can ever think of after this' was the next suggestion (whether by Leigh Hunt or Lamb himself is disputed), 'but without mentioning a name that once put on a semblance of mortality' (as Hazlitt puts it). 'If Shakespeare was to come into this room, we should all rise up to meet him; but if that person was to come into it, we should all fall down and try to kiss the hem of his garment' (Howe, pp.226f., 379). With that, it seems, the meeting broke up.

## The apostolic proclamation

But the starting-point of our present enquiry will not be the miscellaneous tributes of later generations, but the Gospels and the teaching of the apostles themselves. As we saw in the previous chapter, the substance of the apostolic proclamation is clear for all to see. The apostles and their close associates proclaimed Jesus as not only the promised Messiah, but as the eternal 'Word' or Son of God. It was through him that God had created the universe (John 1:1–3; Hebrews 1:2; 1 Corinthians 8:6, Colossians 1:16; *cf.* p.33, above), and he had always been 'one' with the Father; yet he became truly man (John 1:14, 18) and lived a life of constant obedience to the one he habitually addressed as *'Abba'* (my own Father). In this he both revealed the invisible God in the only way we could really begin to understand, and also showed us how man *ought* always to have lived (Colossians 1:15; Hebrews 1:3).

But men had not lived like that; they had sinned and become alienated from God, and our common need was not only revelation but redemption. So when Christ became man he genuinely shared our nature, felt the bitterness of our temptations, and 'learned obedience in the school of suffering' (Hebrews 2:10–18; 5:8, NEB). He never himself sinned (Hebrews 4:15; *cf.* 2 Corinthians 5:21; 1 Peter 2:22; 1 John 3:5), but he identified himself with us so completely that 'in his own person he carried our sins to [or 'on'] the gallows' (1 Peter 2:24, NEB). It could even be said that he was 'made sin' for us (which could be translated 'made a sin offering for us', but probably means rather more than that: namely, that he, the sinless, voluntarily took the sinner's place) in order to reconcile us to God (2 Corinthians 5:21, with verses 18–20). So he died in apparent weakness and shame; but God vindicated him as his Son by raising him from the dead. Now he is exalted as Lord of the universe, and will one day appear again to human eyes – not in weakness but in power, not to suffer but to reign, not as sin-bearer but as judge.

Our task in this chapter is to submit this belief of the apostles and the apostolic church to such examination as we can. How far does it really accord with the picture of

Jesus that emerges from the Gospels? Is that picture itself either false or inconsistent? Does it stand up to criticism? Assuming that the Old Testament records earlier stages of God's self-revelation, does the Gospel picture of Jesus tie in with the Old Testament, and with the way in which the apostolic church interpreted it? And what, if this picture is to be accepted, are its implications?

## The use of metaphors

Before we turn to these questions, we ought to get one possible misunderstanding out of the way. When the early church spoke of Christ 'coming down' from heaven, and then ascending again after the resurrection, was it being childishly naive? Was it obsessed with the concept of a flat earth and a God who was somehow poised above it? If so, does the whole idea become meaningless now that we know that the earth is round, and that what is 'up' in Europe or North America is 'down' in Australia? Would it be better finally to discard any such phrases as 'up there' or 'out there', and not only abandon such picture-language, but also the theological concepts which are alleged to go with them?

Now it is true that in apostolic days, and for many subsequent centuries, everyone did believe that the earth was flat, and did, in all probability, think in terms of a 'three-storeyed' universe. But the New Testament never asserts this as an objective fact, and there is nothing naive about the way in which these terms are used in the New Testament or, indeed, by some people today. I very much doubt if there are many literate adults who do not now realize that what is 'up' in one hemisphere is necessarily 'down' in the other; nor do I believe that the generality of people think of 'heaven' as situated in some particular geographical direction. To teach the young to sing about 'a Friend for little children above the bright blue sky' may be open to minor objections; but what we really mean, if we still sometimes speak of God in terms analogous to his being 'up there' or 'out there', is that he is transcendent as well as immanent.

When, therefore, we read that Jesus said that 'the bread of God is he who comes down from heaven and gives life to the world' (John 6:33) – and then, in an overtly personal reference, that 'I have come down from heaven not to do my will but to do the will of him who sent me' (John 6:38) – he meant that in what we call the incarnation he had come from God and the 'transcendent' world to live a truly human life. Similarly, when we read in Luke 24:51 that 'While he was blessing them, he left them and was taken up into heaven', it means that in what we call the ascension the risen Christ withdrew in a visible way from his disciples to show them that the resurrection appearances of the 'forty days' were at an end. He is now – again to use biblical language – 'Exalted to the right hand of God' (Acts 2:33) and has 'sat down at the right hand of the Majesty in heaven' (Hebrews 1:3): that is, God has raised him to the very throne of the universe. It is clearly impossible to speak about realms and realities far beyond our human experience or understanding without using metaphorical terms and picture language (*cf.* the descriptions of heaven in the book of Revelation). But this does not mean that such language is meaningless, or even naive. And it is very difficult to imagine how Jesus' visible withdrawal from his disciples could have taken a more natural form than that described in Acts 1:9: 'After he said this, he was taken up before their very eyes, and a cloud hid him from their sight.'

Christians, then, do not believe that Jesus simply came from outer space on a temporary visit to this world, and then returned whence he had come – somewhat in the manner of space fiction. They believe that in him God himself (in and through his eternal Son, or Word) came to live a truly human life; that Jesus was not simply God *seeming* to be a man, having assumed a human body and, in part, a human psyche, but actually *becoming* man. I never think of him as 'the God-man' (as some would put it) – for that phrase *suggests* the idea of some sort of hybrid, meta-phorical being, half God and half man. It seems to me far more accurate to think of him as 'God-in-manhood', giving both terms their full force. For in the incarnation One who was essentially God became genuinely man. This is the most stupendous thing that ever happened, so it is no wonder that people boggle at it and question precisely how it could be. We shall look at the evidence for this bald statement later in this chapter – together, of course, with some of its implications. For the present we shall simply insist that to deny that Jesus was truly man is just as false to the New Testament evidence as to deny that he was – and is – truly God.

## The Gospel records

When we turn to the Gospels there can be no doubt whatever about the true humanity of the central figure. He was born as a helpless baby; he grew like any other child; and he experienced hunger, thirst, weariness, pain and death. He could be both angry and deeply grieved; he had infinite compassion for all in need; and he could feel a special affinity with some. He was not omniscient (as on one occasion he stated unequivocally); so he asked questions because he wanted to know the answers, and he repeatedly emphasized that he taught and did nothing that he had not himself been taught by his Father or commanded by him to do. He was tempted just as we are; but the testimony of the New Testament is that he never gave way. The very hallmark of his life was that unswerving obedience to his heavenly Father, and utter dependence on his love and power, which *should* have been the happy experience of all men.

It is true that we never read of him laughing, and that the picture we get is of one so deeply conscious of the sins, sufferings and sorrows of humanity, and so utterly absorbed in doing his Father's will, that he had little time for the lighter side of life. Yet he loved children and understood their games; he was a welcome guest at weddings and parties; he was certainly no 'kill-joy'; and he prayed that his disciples might share the joy that he himself knew. As for humour, I cannot believe that some of the statements he made, or the hyperboles he often used, were not accompanied by a smile on his lips or a twinkle in his eyes.

But although he identified with ordinary people, it is equally obvious from the Gospels that he was himself unique. He was unique in his teaching, his authority, his claims and his sinlessness. Above all, he was unique in the significance of his death and in the fact that God raised him from the grave. But the last two facts, which represent the very heart of the apostles' preaching, are so important that a special chapter must be devoted to each. First, however, we must consider the life that led up to them.

## Jesus' teaching

Before the resurrection he was usually addresssed as 'Teacher'; and what a teacher he was! He seems to have been equally at home when explaining spiritual truths and the good news of the kingdom of God to simple villagers, and when encountering the attacks of theological critics. With his opponents he showed a penetration and quiet incisiveness that staggered them in one who had never studied in any of the rabbinic schools. But what upset them most was his disregard for man-made rules and, still more, the fact that he made claims – sometimes explicit, but more often implicit – which outraged them as tantamount to blasphemy.

Today, those who read the Gospels are, I think, particularly impressed with the *timelessness* of his teaching. Not one of the major sayings attributed to him has become outdated, has been proved false, or has lost its essential relevance when read in a totally different age and environment. We are fascinated by the robust quality of the mind of one who could tell those who warned him of Herod's desire to kill him by saying, 'Go tell that fox, "I will drive out demons and heal people today and tomorrow, and on the third day I will reach my goal"' (Luke 13:31–32); and could also counter a difficult and dangerous intrigue (about the propriety of paying taxes to Rome) by the simple maxim 'Render to Caesar the things that are Caesar's, and to God the things that are God's' (Luke 20:20–26, RSV) – 'a principle which has proved to be the basis of all future discussion on the problem of Church and State'. Nor was his answer on this occasion, as G. B. Caird goes on to say, a 'mere evasion of a verbal trap. It was a messianic manifesto, in which he disavowed all connexion with the Jewish nationalist movement and affirmed his own conviction that it was feasible for Israel to discharge her total commitment to God even as loyal subjects of a pagan empire' (Caird, pp.222f.). No wonder his opponents were 'astonished by his answer'.

One of the most distinctive features of his ministry was the incomparable parables he told. These usually took the form of common episodes in village life (sowing, reaping, fishing, hiring labourers, kneading dough, or appealing to a judge) or stories about absent landlords, servants in debt or entrusted with money, men building houses and kings making war. They aroused general interest, and even the simplest could understand their surface meaning. The spiritually indifferent would leave it at that; but these stories were easy to remember, and many must have mused about their deeper meaning – or even have asked him questions, and joined the inner circle to whom he 'explained everything'.

It is true that there is little that was wholly new in his moral teaching, because the character of God, and his will for his people, had already been set forth in the Old Testament. Jesus was himself 'born under law' (Galatians 4:4) and he kept it faithfully. But he realized that he was inaugurating a new age, for he declared that 'Until John, it was the Law and the prophets: since then, there is the good news of the kingdom of God, and everyone forces his way in' (Luke 16:16, NEB). He had not come to 'destroy' or 'abolish' the Law or the Prophets (Matthew 5:17), but rather to give them 'the particular fulfilment that was always intended', and was 'in each case appropriate' (*cf.* Carson, *Matthew, ad loc.*). Not the least part of the Old Testament was to lose its force until its purposes had been 'accomplished' (Matthew 5:18). So in his teaching he reinforced some of the Old Testament injunctions precisely as they stood. In others he gave them a wider scope, which included not only acts and words but the thoughts and intents of the heart. In some, again, he said that they represented divinely authorized concessions to 'the hardness of [men's] hearts', but did not correspond with God's original intention. And in yet others he made it quite clear that the commandments about ritual cleanness in the Old Testament were soon to give way to the far more vital demands of moral purity (*cf.* Mark 7:1–23). I say 'soon' advisedly, for it was only after his death and resurrection (but clearly before Mark's Gospel was written) that his disciples understood the significance of what he had said.

Such was his teaching in regard to the Old Testament, which he clearly accepted as divinely authoritative, and the prophecies of which he frequently said '*must* be fulfilled'. But he had very little use for the nit-picking regulations with which the written law had been extended by the oral law or 'traditions of the elders'. These made God's law into something too heavy to be born, and frequently led to an oppressive legalism. On some occasions they went so far as actually to evade the intention of the divine Lawgiver and provide a device which even made the fulfilment of that intention illegal (*cf.* the provisions about Corban in Mark 7:9–13). It was for reasons such as these that he denounced the Pharisees and 'teachers of the law' so comprehensively in Matthew 23:13–36. Not all the Pharisees and lawyers were like that, of course, as the New Testament itself makes clear. But it is obvious that Jesus had no time for religious hypocrisy of any sort. To think of him only as 'gentle Jesus, meek and mild' (as a children's hymn puts it) is clearly a caricature. Yet it is good to remember that these stern denunciations in Matthew 23:13–36, with their explicit intimations of judgment to come, are immediately followed by the heart-broken lament:

O Jerusalem, Jerusalem, you who kill the prophets and stone those sent to you, how often I have longed to gather your children together, as a hen gathers her chicks under her wings, but you were not willing. Look, your house is left to you desolate (Matthew 23:37–38).

## His authority

It seems clear that during his earthly life the quality that surprised people most of all was the authority with which he spoke and acted. In Mark 1:22 we read that 'The people were astounded at his teaching, for, unlike the doctors of the law, he taught with a note of authority' (NEB). Just a few verses later, after an exorcism, we read that the people 'were all dumbfounded and began to ask one another, 'What is this? A new kind of teaching! He speaks with authority. When he gives orders, even the unclean spirits submit"'" (verse 27). Even the most cautious critics comment on this quiet, unassuming authority which characterized both his words and deeds.

We hear this note of authority repeatedly, for example, in the 'Sermon on the Mount'. Again and again we read that he started some point of teaching with the words 'You have heard that it was said to the people long ago' (Matthew 5:21, 33), or 'You have heard that it was said' (Matthew 5:27, 38, 43) – or even simply 'It has been said' (Matthew 5:31) – followed in each case by the authoritative 'But I say to you' [or 'tell you'] something different. David Daube regards the thesis, in each case, as corresponding to the rabbinic formula 'I might understand literally', and the antithesis to the rabbinic 'But thou must say' – the latter based either on another text from Scripture or a logical deduction. In rabbinic usage, however, this represents

> academic, dialectic exegesis, with the reason for the preferred view clearly stated; whereas in these verses we have before us, not a scholarly working out by some Rabbis of a progressive interpretation as against a conceivable narrow one, but a laying down by Jesus, supreme authority, of the proper demand.... The setting in life of the rabbinic form is a dialectic exposition of the Law; that of the Matthean is proclamation of the true Law (Daube, pp.57ff.).

True, Daube goes on to say that the Rabbis, in practice, often used this form of argument to combat an interpretation used by others, and to 'substitute a new, freer meaning', but they would never question an accepted dictum openly, as Jesus did, on their personal authority.

Much the same principle applies to the way in which Jesus is reported as so often beginning some important statement with the words, 'Amen, I tell you' (or, in John's Gospel, 'Amen, amen, I tell you' or 'I tell you the truth'). In Jewish usage the term 'Amen' was used at the end of a statement or prayer in the sense of 'So be it' – whether by the speaker himself or by others who were present. Its use to introduce a statement seems to have been peculiar to Jesus, and is noted as characteristic of him by many scholars.[5] In effect it is his substitution for the prophetic 'Thus saith the Lord' or the Old Testament expression 'As I live, saith the Lord', and again echoes the note of authority with which he habitually taught.

As with his teaching, so with his miracles. These should not be regarded as mere portents or marvels, but rather as 'signs' (as John, in particular, describes them) – signs of the compassion he felt for human need, of his will and power to bring relief, and of his willingness to respond to, and confirm, men's faith. We read, of course, of significant miracles also being performed by Moses, by some of the prophets and by the apostles; and the fact that the magicians of Egypt could sometimes match Moses in this (*e.g.* Exodus 7:22), and that some Jews had the power of exorcism (*cf.* Matthew 12:27), shows that what is – or appears to be – supernatural is not necessarily of divine origin (*cf.* 2 Thessalonians 2:9).

Jesus' miracles were, pre-eminently, signs that the kingdom of God, so often spoken of by the Jewish prophets and apocalyptists, had actually come in his person and mission, for he is recorded in Matthew 12:28 as saying: 'if it is by the Spirit of God that I drive out the devils, then be sure that the kingdom of God has already come upon you' (NEB). When that kingdom is consummated, sickness, deformity, evil and death will all be eliminated; so the New Testament miracles are foretastes of what will then be universal. But what distinguishes Jesus' miracles from those of the apostles is not primarily their substance – although some of them seem, indeed, to have been unique – but the fact that the apostles invoked his name on such occasions, while he could and did speak on his own authority.

That last statement is, however, only partially true. For time and again in John's Gospel (which, more than any of the other Gospels, portrays Jesus as the very Son of God) we read that Jesus insisted that 'I do nothing on my own authority, but in all that I say, I have been taught by my Father' (John 8:28, NEB); 'I do not speak on my own authority, but the Father who sent me has himself commanded me what to say and how to speak' (John 12:49, NEB); 'I am not myself the source of the words I speak to

[5] *Cf.* Moule, *Phenomenon*, pp.67f.; Käsemann, pp.41f.; Ladd, p.285; Daube, p.388.

you: it is the Father who dwells in me doing his own work' (John 14:10, NEB). The secret stands revealed in what Dodd termed the 'Parable of the Apprentice' in John 5:19–20 (NEB): 'In truth, in very truth I tell you, the Son can do nothing by himself; he does only what he sees the Father doing: what the Father does, the Son does. For the Father loves the Son and shows him all his works' (or 'all his trade', if we think of Jesus growing up in the carpenter's shop and learning from Joseph – just as, at a very early age, he began to learn directly from the one he knew and recognized as 'Abba').

Almost immediately, the passage continues: 'As the Father raises the dead and gives them life, so the Son gives life to men, as he determines. And again, the Father does not judge anyone, but has given full jurisdiction to the Son; it is his will that all should pay the same honour to the Son as to the Father. To deny honour to the Son is to deny it to the Father who sent him.... For as the Father has life-giving power in himself, so has the Son, by the Father's gift. As Son of Man, he has also been given the right to pass judgment' (John 5:21–27, NEB).

This, then, was the source of his authority – the intimate relationship between Father and Son. This is what explains how one who had truly been made man, and was not omniscient, could speak and teach with absolute authority: for he taught only what the Father had taught him. This, too, was why he could even raise the dead on his own authority, because this authority had been specifically given him. And this was why – although he made it clear that 'God did not send his Son into the world to condemn the world, but to save the world through him' (John 3:17) – he could, and did, go on to say, 'The man who puts his faith in him does not come under judgment; but the unbeliever has already been judged in that he has not given his allegiance to God's only Son. Here lies the test: the light has come into the world, but men preferred darkness to light because their deeds were evil' (John 3:18–19, NEB).

## His claims

### a. In general

It will be seen that our consideration of his authority has inevitably led us into the very heart of his claims. It is true, of course, that Jesus made many other astounding claims during the course of his life and ministry. 'I am the light of the world,' he once said. 'No follower of mine shall wander in the dark; he shall have the light of life' (John 8:12, NEB). 'I am the bread of life,' he said on another occasion. 'Whoever comes to me shall never be hungry, and whoever believes in me shall never be thirsty' (John 6:35, NEB). 'I am the resurrection and I am life,' he told Martha. 'If a man has faith in me, even though he die, he shall come to life; and no one who is alive and has faith shall ever die' (John 11:25–26, NEB). 'Come to me, all you who are weary and burdened,' he said on yet another occasion, 'and I will give you rest. Take my yoke upon you and learn from me, for I am gentle and humble in heart, and you will find rest for your souls. For my yoke is easy and my burden is light' (Matthew 11:28–30).

'Gentle and humble in heart', we read; yet at first sight it does not seem so. We sometimes hear or read statements that assert that Jesus' teaching was *all* about his heavenly Father, and that it was to him alone that he continually bore witness. In a very real sense this is true. Yet, in another sense, it would be almost equally true to say that he was himself the centre of his teaching, and that, rather than point men to any other, he called them to himself. How, then, can these two, apparently contradictory, assessments be reconciled? They find their reconciliation in the very chapter in Matthew's Gospel from which I have just quoted, where Jesus is recorded as saying, 'All things have been committed to me by my Father. No one knows the Son except the Father, and no one knows the Father except the Son and those to whom the Son chooses to reveal him' (Matthew 11:27). In other words, it was only by calling men to himself that he could bring them to a true knowledge of the Father.

## b. In his relationship with the Father

Jesus' consciousness that his filial relationship with the Father was unique must, it seems clear, have dawned upon him at a very early age. Galot, for example, regards the Aramaic word *Abba*, 'the familiar term that Jewish children used to talk to their father' (which he and many other scholars believe Jesus habitually used in prayer in place of the more formal terms in which Jews were wont to address the transcendent 'Father' in heaven), as the key to this unique filial consciousness (Galot, p.155).[6]

Testimony to this unique relationship is by no means confined to Matthew 11:27 and Luke 10:22 in the Synoptic Gospels (to say nothing of the numerous references in John). The earliest Synoptic reference is to be found in the gentle reproach he is recorded as giving to Mary when she expressed her dismay that he had stayed behind in the temple at the age of twelve: 'Didn't you know I had to be in my Father's house?' (Luke 2:49). Further testimony can also be found in the accounts of his baptism and temptation, for Caird persuasively argues that

> the pious ingenuity of the early Church could no more have created these stories than the parables of the Good Samaritan and the Prodigal Son.... The voice from heaven addressed Jesus in a composite quotation from Scripture (Ps. 2:7; Isa. 42:1). Psalm 2 proclaims the accession of the anointed king, who is to rule the nations with a rod of iron. Isa. 42:1–6 is the first of a series of prophesies about the Servant of the Lord, who has been chosen to carry true religion to the Gentiles and who, in achieving this mission, must suffer indignity, rejection and death. Thus the words which he had heard must have meant to Jesus that he was being designated to both these offices... sent out to establish the reign of God, not with the iron sceptre but with patient, self-forgetful

---

[6]Louis Bouyer has suggested that in Jesus' infancy and early childhood 'this consciousness of Jesus, like every normal consciousness, was the consciousness of an object before becoming a consciousness of its own subject. The consciousness of Jesus, as the human consciousness of the Son of God, was before all else consciousness *of God* .... What is unique in the consciousness of Jesus of Nazareth is that it was pierced and traversed, from its first awakening, by that intuition, which was to precede, penetrate, and saturate all his states of consciousness, whatever they might be' (Bouyer, p.510).

service. Remembering Luke's story of the boy Jesus, we cannot suppose that all this now flashed upon him as a new and startling revelation.... The baptism experience represented the end of a long development,...of meditation on the scriptures and of their application to himself (Caird, pp.76f. *Cf.* Matthew 3:17; Mark 1:11; Luke 3:22).

In the temptation which immediately follows, the words of the tempter should almost certainly be translated 'If you really are the Son of God...'. In other words, the temptation was not to doubt this fact, but to presume upon it, and to take a short cut rather than follow the predicted road of suffering.

### c. His messianic mission

It seems equally clear that he identified the concept of the Messiah with that of the 'suffering Servant', rather than with that of the Davidic King and national deliverer in terms of which the Jews commonly thought of him. This explains why he seems carefully to have avoided using this title in his public ministry. But there is strong evidence that he did not repudiate the title when attributed to him in private; the triumphal entry into Jerusalem 'looks uncommonly like a deliberate messianic gesture' (Moule, *Christology*, p.33); and it seems clear that he affirmed the title, whether explicitly or implicitly, when the high priest asked him on oath, 'Are you the Messiah, the Son of the Blessed One?' To this he replied, 'I am [or 'It is as you say']. And you will see the Son of Man sitting at the right hand of the Mighty One and coming on the clouds of heaven' (Mark 14:62). Much has been written by New Testament scholars about the use and meaning of the term 'Son of Man'; but in this verse (in which even C. K. Barrett accepts it as a reference by Jesus to himself) the most important point is that it shows that Jesus saw both the concept of Messiah and that of the 'Son of Man', of whom we read in Daniel 7:13–14, as combined in his own person. It is noteworthy in this whole context that Wolfhart Pannenberg asserts that 'recent study of Jesus has shown, with general agreement, that... the claim of Jesus himself, which is implicitly contained not only in his message but in his whole work, precedes the faith of the disciples' (Pannenberg, p.54). Similarly, in our immediate context, Cullmann insists that 'The early Church believed in Christ's messiahship only because it believed that Jesus believed himself to be Messiah' (Cullmann, p.8).

We must press on to consider the sinlessness of Jesus. But first I want to emphasize the vital point that, even if it could be shown, or persuasively contended, that Jesus did not himself explicitly claim or even accept any particular titles, this would make very little difference to the basic argument. For in point of fact the *implicit* claims of his works and actions speak more clearly than any titles could. As Heinz Zahrnt aptly remarks, it is 'clear that Jesus did not make his status the one, introductory theme of his preaching.... He did not claim a title and thus make his own person the subject of his preaching. He did not say "I am the Messiah", "the Son of God", "the Son of Man", "and because this is what I am, such and such follows and you must believe this and do that..."' (Zahrnt, pp.110f.). On the contrary, he simply spoke with innate authority and let his preaching and his actions speak for themselves. To this we must revert later.

## His sinlessness

We have spoken briefly above about the miracles of Jesus – but at considerably less length than in the first edition of this book. This is chiefly for three reasons. First, because the one-time insistence of scientists on the uniformity of nature and her 'laws' is today much less obtrusive; for physicists, doctors and others have come increasingly to realize that the exceptional and unexpected does happen from time to time, and that cause and effect do not invariably follow the normal pattern. This is not, of course, to open the door to naive credulity, but rather to the principle that all phenomena must be examined on the evidence. Secondly, Jesus was not unique in many of the miracles that he performed, as we have seen:[7] so they cannot be

[7]Except that the apostles made a practice of invoking the name of Jesus, while Jesus always acted and spoke with the personal authority which he knew, and emphasized, that he received direct from the Father.

regarded in themselves as proofs that he was the Son of God. The chief proof of that, as we shall see, is that God raised him from the dead in the way he did. Thirdly, it seems clear that Jesus himself always refused to perform some 'marvel' to convince – or impress – an intellectual dilettante. It was when he met human suffering, or the need to reassure someone who really *wanted* to believe, that he would act in a way to meet their need. To those who have already come to believe on him on other grounds, however, there will be nothing surprising in the fact that he opened blind eyes and deaf ears; that he made the lame walk, the crippled stand upright and the paralytic whole; or even that he raised the dead. These were, as we have seen, 'signs' that in him the promised kingdom of God had indeed come, but had not yet been fully consummated.

We saw earlier in this chapter, moreover, that it is to his moral character that many have pointed as an even greater miracle than anything he did. It has been described as 'sublime', 'divine', 'unique', 'insurpassable' and both 'the highest pattern of virtue' and 'the strongest incentive to its practice'. But to assert that he, alone among all men, was 'sinless' is to go very much further still. In a real sense, moreover, it simply cannot be *proved*, for it is impossible to prove a negative. To begin with, the record of his life, teaching and character in the Gospels represents no more than a fraction of what could have been reported, as John's Gospel itself makes clear in the words: 'There is much else that Jesus did. If it were all to be recorded in detail, I suppose the whole world would not hold the books that would be written' (John 21:25, NEB). Above all, as has often been remarked, how are we to know the thoughts that may not only have presented themselves to his heart and mind (for that is not sin; instead, it is the very stuff and substance of temptation), but might perhaps have found even a temporary harbour?

All that we can do is to assess the evidence. First, there is the testimony of those who knew him best. 'He committed no sin, and no deceit was found in his mouth,' Peter wrote of him (1 Peter 2:22, echoing Isaiah 53:9), and then continued: 'When they hurled their insults at him, he did not retaliate; when he suffered, he made no threats. Instead, he entrusted himself to him who judges justly' – in which the present participles and imperfect tenses of the Greek emphasize a continuing attitude and may well point to the way in which Peter as an eyewitness was recalling the actual event (1 Peter 2:22–23). Put more briefly, John states that 'Christ appeared, as you know, to do away with sins, and there is no sin in him' (1 John 3:5, NEB). And the Fourth Gospel records that on one occasion Jesus rounded on his critics and challenged them with the question 'Can any of you prove me guilty of sin?' (John 8:46), and, on another, declared that Satan 'has no hold on me' (John 14:30).

But the testimony at this point goes much deeper than any isolated statement, for it rests on the fact that the records give no hint whatever that he had any personal consciousness of sin – or even forgiven sin. As C. E. Jefferson justly remarks:

> The best reason we have for believing in the sinlessness of Jesus is the fact that He allowed His dearest friends to think that He was. There is in all His talk no trace of regret or hint of compunction, or suggestion of sorrow for shortcoming, or slightest vestige or remorse. He taught other men to think of themselves as sinners, He asserted plainly that the human heart is evil, He told His disciples that every time they prayed they were to pray to be forgiven, but He never speaks or acts as though He Himself has the slightest consciousness of having ever done anything other than what was pleasing to God (Jefferson, p.225).

To appreciate the full significance of this fact we must contrast the inner consciousness of Jesus with that of those men and women whom we rightly regard as saints. It seems to be their unanimous testimony that the further they progress in the inner life, and the nearer they get to God, the more conscious they become of their own unworthiness. Imperfections which were once tolerable or even unnoticed become black, ugly and abhorrent in the light of their deeper apprehension of the divine holiness. Yet in him there is a total absence of any such experience. On the contrary, we find from time to time unselfconscious references to his holiness, humility and meekness. And Griffith Thomas pertinently observes that this

> is the more remarkable if we observe the instances in the life of Jesus when he expressed indignation against his enemies.... With every other man the expression of indignation tends to a subsequent feeling of compunction, or, at any rate, to a close examination whether there may not have been some element of personal animosity or injustice in the expression of anger. But with Jesus Christ there was nothing of the kind. Not for a single instant did the faintest shadow come between Him and His heavenly Father (Thomas, p.16).

All this is largely negative – the inability of his opponents to bring any moral accusation against him, even at his trial; the failure of his closest friends to see any flaw in his character or behaviour; and the fact that one who has, all down the ages, made others feel conscious of their sins and unworthiness, seems to have had no such consciousness himself. But could he have been so insensitive as to sin without knowing it? Let us briefly examine some of the accusations that have, at times, been brought against him.

## Some alleged blemishes

### a. The Gentile woman

In this incident, recorded in Matthew 15:21–28 and Mark 7:24–30, a Gentile woman brought to Jesus a daughter 'possessed by an evil spirit' and besought his help. At first he did not answer her, saying to his disciples 'I was sent only to the lost sheep of Israel' (Matthew 15:23–24). Then he said to the woman: 'First let the children eat all they want, for it is not right to take the children's bread and toss it to their [pet] dogs' (Mark 7:27; *cf.* Cranfield, p.249). To this the woman promptly replied 'Yes Lord, but even the dogs under the table eat the children's crumbs' (Mark 7:28) – and Jesus said, 'Woman, you have great faith! Your request is granted' (Matthew 15:28).

This episode has prompted two accusations: that Jesus was arrogant and insensitive to her in the words he used, and that he was narrow and race-bound in his sympathies. But it seems highly probable that the tone of his voice, and possibly a twinkle in his eye, must have encouraged her instant and witty reply. It is true that at first he appeared to be unwilling to extend his ministry of teaching and mercy beyond the race in which he had been born and to which he had primarily been sent. No doubt there is a limited sense in which this was true; he had come with a specific ministry to which he consistently gave priority. But it is perfectly clear that his sympathies flowed much more widely than this – as can be seen in the parable of the Good Samaritan (Luke 10:29–37); in his healing of the centurion's servant, and his commendation of the former's faith (Matthew 8:5–10); in his assertion that many would come from east and west and sit down in the kingdom of heaven, while the children of the kingdom might be cast out (Matthew 8:11–12); in his reference to the 'other' sheep, not of 'this fold', whom he must also win (John 10:16); and in his commission to his disciples to take his message to 'every creature' or 'the whole creation' (Mark 16:15; *cf*. Matthew 28:19). Surely, then, we are entitled to interpret a single incident – about which we have no more than a bare summary – in the light of his consistent attitude and teaching.

### b. The herd of pigs

I myself find more difficulty in understanding the notable exorcism which involved the destruction of some 2,000 pigs, the story of which is recorded in Matthew 8:28–34, Mark 5:1–20 and Luke 8:26–37. The well-known differences between the manuscripts which locate the exorcism 'in the region of the Gadarenes', the 'Gerasenes' and the 'Gergesenes', respectively, need not detain us here, and I shall follow Metzger in accepting 'Gadarenes' as the best reading. Nor do I find any real difficulty in the fact that Matthew mentions two wild, demon-possessed men, while Mark and Luke mention one only, since it is common practice at times to confine an account of some incident to the principal person (or spokesman) concerned, and at others to mention some companion also, as Matthew does on more than one occasion. The basic difficulty in understanding this incident is that we know so little about demons in general and demon-possession in particular. Many people, of course, dismiss the whole subject today as mere superstition or a primitive explanation of psychiatric or epileptic disorders, while others are all too ready to resort to exorcism where there is no real evidence of demon-possession. The phenomenon itself seems to be world-wide, sometimes deliberately sought by shamans, witch-doctors or mediums. In civilized countries it appears to be rare, except among those who have rashly dabbled in the occult; but many missionaries have at times encountered it. It seems to have been unusually widespread during the life of Christ, but it is very seldom mentioned in the rest of the Bible. So it has been plausibly suggested that, after the temptation in the desert, this phenomenon represented a calculated challenge to his authority.

It is noteworthy that on many occasions we are told that the demons recognized Jesus' real status and knew that, when his kingdom was consummated, their judgment would come; and on this occasion that they feared he had come 'to torment us before our time'. Desiring, apparently, some sort of embodiment, they begged that, when forced to come out of the men, they might be allowed to go into a large herd of pigs grazing in the vicinity – and Jesus 'gave them leave'. The result was that the pigs rushed over a precipice into the sea and were drowned. What happened then to the demons we do not know: presumably they went to what they termed 'the Abyss'. Nor do we know whether Jesus himself knew what the result of their entering into the pigs would be – for, although he repeatedly told his disciples that what he did and taught was *only* what was commanded by his Father (and therefore absolutely authoritative), the incarnate Lord was not omniscient. So the moral criticism levelled against Jesus personally, that he 'deliberately' caused the pigs to die what was, presumably, a speedy death, and their owners to suffer considerable financial loss, may indeed be wholly misplaced. Taken as an act of God, moreover, it should not, I think, be regarded as a judgment on their owners for keeping pigs contrary to the Jewish law, for the district was predominantly Gentile, but rather as a striking demonstration that human beings are of much more value than God's other creatures, and that man's salvation is infinitely more important than financial profit or loss.

## c. The 'cleansing' of the temple and 'cursing' of the fig-tree

Another criticism that has been brought against Jesus is that of petulance, or even high-handedness, in his cleansing of the temple and his cursing of the barren fig-tree. But little difficulty need be felt in regard to the first of these, at any rate. On the contrary, there was nothing petty or personal in his indignation, which was aroused exclusively by the fact that the priests, the money-changers and their henchmen were putting his 'Father's house' to such a sordid use. Instead of its being 'a house of prayer for all nations' (Isaiah 56:7), they were turning it into 'a den of robbers' (Jeremiah 7:11). They were exploiting the poor, and indulging their own greed, by forcing worshippers to buy special animals provided at exorbitant rates for sacrifice and to change 'Gentile' coins into the only currency they would accept in the temple. This not only made a place designed for worship into one of commerce, but served as a continual reminder that 'Gentile coins, as well as Gentile persons, were intolerable to the Jews in their temple' (Marsh, p.158). No wonder he 'made a whip out of cords, and drove all from the temple area, both sheep and cattle; he scattered the coins of the money changers and overturned their tables. To those who sold doves he said, "Get these out of here! How dare you turn my Father's house into a market!"' (John 2:15–16). This was an act of righteous judgment, as his disciples realized when they 'remembered that it was written, "Zeal for your house will consume me."' Contrary to the statement of one commentary I have read, there is no evidence whatever that he 'inflicted blows on the guilty'. But it certainly cannot be denied that he acted with a degree of 'violence' to rebuke a public evil.

The case of the barren fig-tree is rather different – although, significantly enough, it comes in Mark's Gospel immediately after the cleansing of the temple. Manson goes so far as to state that the Marcan account 'is a tale of miraculous power wasted in the service of ill-temper (for the supernatural energy employed to blast the unfortunate tree might have been more usefully expended in forcing a crop of figs out of season)'. So he concludes that 'as it stands' this story is 'simply incredible' – words which I would refer, instead, to the way in which he treats the whole incident.[8] The true meaning, surely, is that this was an enacted *parable of judgment* – performed not on man or beast, but on an insentient tree. On this interpretation it becomes a matter of little significance whether Jesus, as many commentators insist, might have expected to find *some* fruit, however premature and unripe, which 'usually appeared on a fig tree [even] *before* the leaves' (Tasker, p.201). This may be so. But the important point is that Jesus seems to 'have used his hunger as an occasion for instructing his disciples. That is not to say that he expected to find edible figs.... But that Jesus should look for fruit on a tree at a season when there was no chance of there being any is exactly the sort of thing we should expect, if this was a parabolic action; for an element of the unexpected and the incongruous, which would stimulate curiosity, was a characteristic feature of the symbolic actions of the O.T. prophets (*e.g.* Jer. 13:1ff.; 19:1ff.).... A people which honoured God with their lips but whose heart was far from him (Mark 7:6) was like a tree with an abundance of leaves but no fruit' (Cranfield, pp.356f.).

## d. Divine judgment in general

But was Jesus right to believe – as he certainly did – in a God who loves sinners but hates their sin; who is 'light', in the sense of utter moral purity, as well as 'love'; who is ready to go to incredible lengths to save men from misery and sin, yet cannot tolerate evil, or act as though it did not exist? It is clear from the Gospels that Jesus not infrequently spoke about both judgment and hell; that Matthew records that he once predicted that a day would come when he would send his angels to 'weed out of his kingdom everything that causes sin and all who do evil', and to 'throw them into the fiery furnace, where there will be weeping and gnashing of teeth' (Matthew 13:41–42); and that he spoke in much the same way on a number of occasions. No doubt much of what he said on this subject was in figurative

[8]*Cf.* Manson, p.279.

terms, for how can the glories of fellowship with the living God in 'heaven', or the agony of being excluded from his presence in 'hell', be described in other than picture language (*cf.* the book of Revelation)? But it is frankly *perverse*, in my view, to suggest with Bertrand Russell that Jesus felt 'a certain pleasure in contemplating wailing and gnashing of teeth' (Russell, p.23). This would be wholly out of character in one who said he had come 'to seek and to save what was lost' (Luke 19:10), 'not to call the righteous, but sinners' (Matthew 9:13), and who said that he was 'the good shepherd' who would 'lay down [his] life for the sheep' (John 10:14–15). On the contrary, these words of solemn warning were spoken in the same spirit as his lament over Jerusalem: 'O Jerusalem, Jerusalem, you who kill the prophets and stone those sent to you, how often I have longed to gather your children together, as a hen gathers her chicks under her wings, but you were not willing' (Matthew 23:37). In the final analysis, whether he was right to speak such searing words of warning entirely depends, of course, on whether our God is a God of judgment as well as love. And to this the whole Bible bears testimony.

## e. His denunciations of the 'scribes and Pharisees'

Much the same considerations apply to the severity with which he denounced the 'teachers of the law' and the Pharisees as a class. These denunciations should not, of course, be regarded as by *any* means all-inclusive: witness Nicodemus, Joseph of Arimathea, the lawyer to whom he said 'You are not far from the kingdom of God' (Mark 12:34) and – no doubt – many others. Nor were the severe criticisms which Matthew seems to have collected together in chapter 23 occasioned by any hostile reaction to their treatment of him personally; they were evoked by the pain and anger he always felt when he came face to face with religious hypocrisy, with those who tried to impose on others standards of behaviour much higher than their own, whose legal niceties led them to 'strain out a gnat but swallow a camel', and whose teachings 'shut the kingdom of heaven in men's faces'. But it was, indeed, the obduracy of the 'chief priests and elders of the people' that prompted his sad comments in Matthew 21:31–32: 'I tell you the truth, the tax collectors and the prostitutes are entering the kingdom of God ahead of you. For John came to you to show you the way of righteousness, and you did not believe him, but the tax collectors and the prostitutes did. And even after you saw this, you did not repent and believe him.'

*f. His 'failure' to denounce social and economic injustice*

Jesus has also been accused of being insufficiently concerned with political, social and economic questions, and having done little to combat, or even to denounce, contemporary social evils such as slavery, the status of women, and widespread injustice. But it is clear from the Sermon on the Mount that he was deeply concerned that his disciples should be both the 'salt' and the 'light' of secular society; he endorsed the authority of those Old Testament prophets who vehemently rebuked social injustice; and he consistently identified himself with the poor and weak, with social outcasts and those who were regarded as morally disreputable. In Dietrich Bonhoeffer's striking phrase, he was 'the man for others', who had come not to be served but to serve, and whose basic mission was to all who were 'lost'. It is true that he did not lead a rebellion against Rome, seek to free slaves, or introduce a social revolution. He had come for a particular purpose, which was far more important than any of these things – and from that purpose nothing could or did deflect him. He was primarily concerned to change men as men rather than the political regime under which they lived; to transform their atttude rather than their circumstances; to treat the sickness of their hearts rather than the problems of their environment. But the paramount emphasis he always put on the ancient command, 'love your neighbour as yourself' (Leviticus 19:18), is apparent not only from repeated references in the Gospels, but also from the ethical teaching of Paul (Romans 13:9–10; Galatians 5:4) and James (2:8); and the wholly new scope he gave to the concept of 'neighbour' is vividly illustrated by the parable of the Good Samaritan (Luke 10:29–37). It is certainly not Jesus' fault that the Christian church has been so slow, and often unwilling (all down the centuries), to apply this principle in an honest and sacrificial way to racial, social and economic problems.

## Personal traits

One of the most remarkable things about him was the perfect balance of character he displayed. It is a truism that a man's strong points nearly always carry with them corresponding weaknesses. He may be an extrovert or an introvert; he may be sanguine or melancholic, choleric or phlegmatic; or he may in some degree combine two or three of these temperaments. But he never succeeds in achieving a perfect balance – a sympathy which is never weak, a strength which is never insensitive, a benevolence which is never indulgent, or a drive which is never ruthless. Jesus, alone, seems to have achieved this balance; and in him every temperament finds both its ideal and its correction. He was a man, not a woman, yet women as much as men find their perfect example in him. He was a Jew, not a European, African or Indian; yet men and women of every race find in him all they would most wish to be.

One of those features which Professor Moule considers to carry the hallmark of authenticity in the Gospels is Jesus' attitude to women and his relations with them. 'It is difficult enough for anyone, even a consummate master of imaginative writing,' he remarks, 'to create a picture of a deeply pure, good person moving about in an impure environment, without making him a prig or a prude or a sort of "plaster saint". How comes it that, through all the Gospel traditions without exception, there comes a remarkably firmly-drawn portrait of an attractive young man moving freely about among women of all sorts, including the decidedly disreputable, without a trace of sentimentality, unnaturalness, or prudery, and yet, at every point, maintaining a simple integrity of character? Is this because the environments in which the traditions were preserved and through which they were transmitted were peculiarly favourable to such a portrait? On the contrary, it seems that they were rather hostile to it' (Moule, *Phenomenon*, pp.63ff.).

Again, he clearly loved children, understood their games and frequently used them as illustrations. When he wanted to emphasize the humility and simple trust that must characterize those who accept his kingly rule, for example, he 'called a little child and had him stand among them. And he said: "I tell you the truth, unless you change and become like little children, you will never enter the kingdom of heaven. Therefore, whoever humbles himself like this child is the greatest in the kingdom of heaven"' (Matthew 18:2–4). On another occasion, commenting on the fact that whatever he did provoked criticism, he said: 'To what can I compare the people of this day? They are like children sitting in the market-place. One group shouts to the other, "We played wedding music for you, but you wouldn't dance! We sang funeral songs, but you wouldn't cry!" When John came, he fasted and drank no wine, and everyone said, "He has a demon in him!" When the Son of Man came, he ate and drank, and everyone said, "Look at this man! He is a glutton and a drinker, a friend of tax collectors and other outcasts!"' (Matthew 11:16–19, GNB). But this carping criticism seems to have had no effect whatever on either his manner of life or his peace of mind. He was happy to accept invitations from people with whom the Pharisees would avoid every possible contact, for he wanted to inculcate the fact, but by precept and practice, that 'People who are well do not need a doctor, but only those who are sick. Go and find out what is meant by the scripture that says: "It is kindness that I want, not animal sacrifices." I have not come to call respectable people, but outcasts' (Matthew 9:12–13, GNB). And his attitude was much the same in the case of the woman caught in the act of committing adultery whom the Pharisees brought to him for judgment. 'If any one of you is without sin, let him be the first to throw a stone at her,' he said. Then, when they all, one by one, slunk away, he asked her: 'Has no-one condemned you?' 'No-one sir,' she said. 'Then neither do I condemn you,' Jesus declared. 'Go now and leave your life of sin' (John 8:3–11).

Yet he could be devastating when face to face with those who put their own traditions before the commandments of God. On one occasion, we are told, 'the Pharisees and teachers of the law asked Jesus, "Why don't your disciples live according to the tradition of the elders instead of eating

their food with 'unclean' hands [that is, without a ceremonial washing]?"' But he rounded on them and said that
Isaiah had been right 'when he prophesied about you
hypocrites; as it is written: "These people honour me with
their lips, but their hearts are far from me. They worship
me in vain; their teachings are but rules taught by men"'
(Mark 7:5–7; *cf.* Isaiah 29:13). Then he instanced the clever
legal device by which they allowed a man to tell his father
or mother that 'Whatever help you might otherwise have
received from me is Corban' (that is, a gift devoted to God).
After saying this it was not only permissible, but legally
incumbent, for the person to break the clear-cut command
of God that he should 'honour' his father or mother (by
providing financial support). After this example, Jesus
called the crowd to him and said: 'Listen to me, everyone,
and understand this. Nothing outside a man can make him
"unclean" by going into him. Rather, it is what comes out of
a man that makes him "unclean"' (Mark 7:10–15).

But this saying was too much even for his disciples to
understand; so, as with many of his 'parables', he had to
explain it. 'Are you so dull?' he asked. 'Don't you see that
nothing that enters a man from the outside can make him
"unclean"? For it doesn't go into his heart but into his
stomach, and then out of his body.' Instead, it is 'what
comes out of a man that makes him "unclean". For from
within, out of men's hearts, come evil thoughts, sexual
immorality, theft, murder, adultery, greed, malice, deceit,
lewdness, envy, slander, arrogance and folly' (Mark
7:17–22). Thus he put the whole emphasis of his teaching
on moral purity rather than ceremonial 'cleanness' – and
thereby (as was realized by the time when Mark's Gospel
was written) he made it clear that all the ritual regulations
of the Mosaic law had fulfilled their purpose, and were no
longer incumbent.

## What do you think about the Messiah?

In conclusion, then, we come back to the question Jesus
himself put to those who had been testing him with difficult
questions. 'What do you think about the Christ?' he asked.
'Whose son is he?' To this they gave the answer that almost

any Jew of that time would have given and replied, 'The son of David.' 'How then', he asked them, 'is it that David, speaking by the Spirit, calls him "Lord"?' and he quoted Psalm 110:1. This question and answer (in Matthew 22:42–45) goes far towards explaining why Jesus avoided claiming the title of Messiah in his public ministry, because it would have been misunderstood. As Caird comments (in reference to the same incident as recorded in Luke 20:44):

> We need not suppose that Jesus was denying his descent from David, which the New Testament elsewhere abundantly affirms . . . . Nor is it likely that he regarded Davidic descent as totally irrelevant to the status of the Messiah . . . . He means that the Son of David is, by itself, an inadequate and misleading description of the Messiah, and that the Old Testament contains intimations that the Coming One will be a far more exalted figure who, instead of merely occupying the throne of David, will share the throne of God (Caird, p.226).

The Old Testament does, indeed, contain such intimations. So, in deciding on our own answer to this vital question – on which our whole future destiny may depend – we must take into account three different, but concurring, strands of evidence: the Old Testament predictions, the New Testament records, and the controversies (and conclusions) of the Christian church.

### a. The Old Testament predictions

As we have seen, the Jews in Jesus' day were looking forward to the coming of their promised Messiah as 'the son of David' who would deliver Israel from her oppressors, restore the glories of Zion and rule in righteousness (*cf.* Psalms 45:3–7; 72:1–4; Isaiah 11:1–5). But the prophesies in fact went much farther than this, for they included many predictions that he would be more than *purely* human. His sway was to be not only universal (Psalm 2:8) but eternal (Isaiah 9:7), and even divine (Psalm 45:6–7). The prophet Micah speaks of his pre-existence (Micah 5:2); Jeremiah describes him as 'The LORD Our Righteousness' (Jeremiah

23:6); and Isaiah speaks of him as 'Wonderful Counsellor, Mighty God, Everlasting Father, Prince of Peace' (Isaiah 9:6). These predictions, which could be multiplied, are the more remarkable in the light of the rigid – and almost mathematical – monotheism which characterizes the Old Testament revelation of God; so it is clearly a matter for wonder that H. P. Liddon could justly speak of 'those successive predictions of a Messiah personally distinct from Jehovah, yet also the Saviour of men, the Lord and Ruler of all, the Judge of the nations, Almighty, Everlasting, nay, One whom prophecy designates as God' (Liddon, p.96). And it is interesting in this context to note that the statement in Hebrews 1:6 ('And again, when God brings his firstborn into the world, he says, "Let all God's angels worship him"') almost certainly represents a quotation taken from the 'Septuagint' Greek version of the Old Testament of words omitted from the end of Deuteronomy 32:43 in the now official Hebrew or 'Massoretic' text, but present in that of the Dead Sea Scrolls.

## b. The New Testament records

Yet when, in the fullness of time, the Messiah (to whose coming these, and many other, prophecies referred) actually came, it might at first sight have seemed almost an anticlimax. It is true that we have two simple, factual accounts of the fact that he was supernaturally conceived. But the virgin birth does not even begin to rank with the resurrection in the preaching and teaching of the New Testament. Alan Richardson is right, however, when he observes that 'two frequently alleged objections' to belief in the virgin birth 'can be discounted at once':

First, it is said that virgin-births are common in all pagan religions and that it was inevitable that when Christ came to be supposed divine, he should be deemed to be born of a virgin. This statement, however, is false: pagan mythology is full of legends of a supernatural hero born of intercourse between a god and a human woman. But this is scarcely *virgin* birth, and there is no real parallel to the story of the birth of Christ in pagan literature. The Jewish mind (and Matt. 1 and Luke 1 are intensely Jewish)

would have been revolted by the idea of physical intercourse between a divine being and a woman. Secondly,
it is alleged that the belief in the Virgin Birth of Christ
arose from a morbid notion of sexual intercourse as
sinful and therefore unacceptable as the means of the
incarnation of the holy God. But again this morbid notion
of sexuality is totally absent from the Jewish mind in
general and from the birth narratives of the Gospels in
particular. If we are looking for motives which would
account for the 'invention' of a legend of the Virgin Birth,
it could more plausibly be found in the desire of the
Gospel-writers to stress the reality of Christ's humanity
as one who was truly born of a woman, like other men, as
over against incipient adoptionist and Gnostic notions
that he was not really a man at all but only a play-acting
divine manifestation (Richardson, p.357).

His boyhood was – outwardly at least – perfectly normal.
To this the only exception was that intimate knowledge of
God as 'Abba' (my own Father) which, as we have seen,
seems to have dawned upon him at a very early age and to
have shown itself when, at the age of twelve, he was surprised that his mother should not have realized that she
would find him in 'my Father's house'. Christmas hym-
nology which suggests that he never cried in his cradle is
nonsense; for how else could a baby let his mother know
that he was hungry or uncomfortable? Yet his sinlessness
must have shown itself (normally, no doubt, in unnoticed
ways) even in early childhood. But in every other way he
grew up – as the Gospels indicate, and the Epistle to the
Hebrews expressly declares – 'like his brothers in every
way' (Hebrews 2:17), sharing their humanity and mortality
(2:14), 'tempted in every way, just as we are' (4:15), learning
obedience in the school of suffering (5:8) and thus attaining
to *human* perfection of character (2:10).

As we know from the Gospels, his prayers normally took
the form of tranquil communion and fellowship with
'Abba'. But on at least one occasion he 'offered up prayers
and petitions with loud cries and tears to the one who could
save him from death, and he was heard because of his
reverent submission' (Hebrews 5:7). We know from the

Gospels about the agony of his prayer and petitions, and the wonder of his complete submission to 'Abba, Father', in the garden of Gethsemane as he contemplated the physical and (above all) the spiritual horror of the crucifixion (*cf.* Mark 14:34–36 and parallels). We also know of the subsequent cry of desolation from the cross – the only time, apparently, when he addressed his Father simply as 'My God, my God' (Mark 15:34) – followed, when the darkness of desolation was over, by the triumphant cry 'Finished!' (John 19:30) and the final prayer, 'Father, into your hands I commit my spirit' (Luke 23:46). But to this subject of the inevitability of the Roman gallows we shall devote our next chapter. What concerns us here is his humanity, and the costliness of his obedience.

I mentioned above in passing that there was just *one* respect in which he could not have been 'tempted in every way, just as we are' – namely, that of sliding yet again down the very slippery slope of some sin into which we have fallen so often in the past. But that one exception is covered by our verse (Hebrews 4:15), which ends with the words 'yet was without sin' (words which could in fact be translated 'sin apart'). Yet that does not mean that his temptations were in any way less bitter and exacting than ours – although it might at first thought appear so. The fact is that if temptation was devastatingly strong we should all, sooner or later, give way – were it not for the gracious promise in 1 Corinthians 10:13 that 'God is faithful; he will not let you be tempted beyond what you can bear. But when you are tempted, he will also provide a way out' (*not* 'a way of escape') 'so that you can stand up under it'. It is only the one who *never* sinned who has been allowed to taste the very depths of temptation.

But, someone may object, didn't he know that he was ultimately invulnerable – and wouldn't that have drawn the sting of any temptation? No, I do not believe that he went into temptation with an in-built sense of invulnerability. I believe he went into temptation, as all else, in complete dependence on his Father. And it is clear that his Father allowed him — pre-eminently in the desert, in Gethsemane and on the cross – to be tempted to the very depths. That is why he is supremely able to sympathize with us, and also – as we shall see – not only to extend to us mercy for the past and grace for our present time of need (Hebrews 4:16), but even to 'save us to the uttermost' (Hebrews 7:25).

Yet, alongside this full humanity of the incarnate life, we must also remember the claims (explicit, and still more implicit) that he made, some of which his compatriots (justly, on their mistaken view of his person) regarded as rank blasphemy. After all, who would ever think of crucifying the 'gentle Jesus, meek and mild' of the liberal Protestantism of the past? He claimed to be 'Lord even of the Sabbath' (Mark 2:28), and we know what the Sabbath meant to the Pharisees and lawyers. He said that he had come 'to give his life as a ransom for many' (Mark 10:45). He stated that 'All things have been committed to me by my Father . . . and no one knows the Father except the Son and those to whom the Son chooses to reveal him' (Matthew 11:27). He even claimed to have the power to forgive sins (Mark 2:2–12 and parallels; Luke 7:48); and every Jew knew that the forgiveness of sins was a divine prerogative. It is a complete caricature to picture him, as some have, 'strutting about the world proclaiming that he was God'. But it is undeniable that, in complete accordance with his Father's will, he frequently both acted and spoke in a way that was appropriate for God alone. He could even say that 'Anyone who has seen me has seen the Father', for 'it is the Father, living in me, who is doing his work' (John 14:9–10). As C. S. Lewis put it:

> The historical difficulty of giving for the life, sayings and influence of Jesus any explanation that is not harder than the Christian explanation, is very great. The discrepancy between the depth and sanity and (let me add) *shrewdness* of His moral teaching and the rampant megalomania which must lie behind His theological teaching unless He is indeed God, has never been satisfactorily got over. Hence the non-Christian hypotheses succeed each other with the restless fertility of bewilderment (Lewis, *Miracles,* p.113).

## c. *The controversies and conclusions of the church*

For all the wonder of Jesus' character, life and teaching, it was not until God raised him from the dead (as we have seen) that the disciples began to understand who their Master really was. Suddenly, as it were, they felt free to worship him, to pray to him, to call him Lord. Without any doctrine of the Trinity, they instinctively began to identify Jesus, in some sense they did not fully understand, with the covenant God of their fathers. And the day of Pentecost brought them yet another experience of God which made the risen and ascended Jesus mean more to them than their previous fellowship with him had ever meant. Naturally enough, therefore, fellow Jews began to challenge them as to whether they were still monotheists. This explains why the church was faced with debates about the nature of the Godhead even before the detailed debates that supervened about how Jesus could be both God and man. It also goes far to explain why they tended to reason 'from above' – from their concept of the Godhead to Jesus of Nazareth – rather than 'from below' – from what they knew of Jesus as a man to his relationship with God.

Much controversy ensued, some of it based on the categories of Greek philosophy and some on the personality of those primarily concerned. Eventually the bounds of what was regarded as orthodoxy were delineated, in AD 451, by the 'Definition of Chalcedon'. This affirmed that 'our Lord Jesus Christ' was, and is, both 'truly God and truly man', 'of one substance with the Father' as to his Godhead, and with us as to his manhood: one Person, with two natures. Even so, controversy continued – not only among those who rejected the Definition, but also among those who interpreted it in different ways. For example, one school of thought, based largely on Alexandria, emphasized his essential deity so strongly that, while they maintained the integrity of his Person, they put his genuine humanity at risk. Another school, centred chiefly on Antioch, emphasized his two natures to such an extent as to endanger the integrity of his Person. They pictured Jesus as acting sometimes as God and at others as man in a way that almost suggests schizophrenia – whereas the Jesus of the Gospels was an essentially integrated person.

But isn't all this very recondite, and of little importance to the layman? This is true, I think, of some of the details, and of the reasoning behind them. But the central fact – that Jesus was truly God but was genuinely 'made man' – is of absolutely vital importance. For if Jesus was not essentially 'one' with the Father, then his death could never have saved us from our sins or even have proved God's own love for us, as we shall see in our next chapter; and his resurrection would not have meant that we now have a divine Saviour, who has opened up heaven for us and will preserve us – and even make us fit – for its enjoyment. But if, on the other hand, he had not truly become man – in the full sense we have seen spelt out in the Epistle to the Hebrews – he could not have provided us with the perfect human example to which we must always aspire, and he could not be the Friend and Leader who can sympathize with the trials, sorrows and temptations – as well as the joys – of human life, and can represent us as our Advocate before the throne of God.

I have discussed elsewhere[9] some of the more detailed problems connected with the biblical teaching about the incarnation – whether those that have been debated down the centuries or those that have featured more particularly in recent books on this subject. But no consideration of the historical evidence for Christianity or for the person and relevance of its Founder can be other than wholly inadequate unless or until it faces up to the fact and the meaning of his death on a Roman gibbet and the church's subsequent conviction that his lifeless body has been raised from mortality to immortality, from the perishable to the imperishable. So it is to these two subjects that we must now turn.

[9]*Cf.* Norman Anderson, *The Mystery of the Incarnation.*

# 3
# The Roman gibbet: was it inevitable?

*The crucifixion: a fact of history · But did Jesus die on the cross? · Why was Jesus crucified? · Why was his death seen in retrospect as inevitable? · The divine necessity for the cross · Interpretations: a. The subjective or 'humanistic' · b. The 'classical' or 'dramatic' · c. The 'juridical' or 'Latin' · Conclusion*

## The crucifixion: a fact of history

In our consideration of the central figure which dominates the New Testament we have hitherto paid little attention either to his death or to his alleged resurrection, since each of these was to be the subject of a special study. An examination of the evidence for resurrection as physical fact rather than beautiful myth, however, is an essential component in any discussion of the historical basis for the Christian faith or of the view we must take of Christ himself. In regard to the crucifixion, on the other hand, the major question which confronts us is different. Here we are not primarily concerned with its historicity, but its explanation; not so much with whether it happened, but why it happened. As Otto Betz puts it:

The fundamental fact to which the quest of the historical Jesus always brings us back is his death on the cross. Nowadays the liberal scholar is sometimes reproached with having no adequate explanation for this fact. How could the devout and lovable teacher of a higher morality possibly have been crucified? . . . . Why should a prophet and rabbi, a 'voice before the end', be more deserving of the cross than the liberal teacher of a higher ethic? It is not enough to point to Jesus' conflict with the Pharisees and the sovereign manner in which he dealt with the Law . . . . For no Jewish heretic ever died on the cross.[1]

Now of the fact that Jesus was crucified there would seem to be virtually no room for any serious debate. A. E. Harvey, for example, has recently committed himself to the statement that 'it may be said that there are few facts which come to us from the ancient world so well attested as the statement that Jesus was crucified' (Harvey, p.50). To doubt this fact would be virtually tantamount to questioning the historicity of Jesus himself and of everything reported about him; and we have already noted the overwhelming evidence against any such suggestion. All our ancient sources without exception – Roman, Jewish, Christian and secondary – testify to the fact that he was crucified, many of them adding words to the effect that this was 'under Pontius Pilate'.

In the case of the Jews it would, no doubt, be possible to argue that they had a powerful motive to stress (or even, in theory, to invent) the fact that this was the way in which Jesus had been executed. This is because it would certainly reinforce their opposition to any tendency to regard him as Messiah. They would be able to insist that the statement in Deuteronomy 21:23, that 'anyone who is hung on a tree is under God's curse', must be regarded as a decisive rebuttal of the suggestion that Jesus was Messiah. To the Romans, on the other hand, it would merely be a common-place mention of a historical fact. It had no other significance

---

[1]Betz, p.83. On the statement that 'no Jewish heretic ever died on the cross' he adds, in a footnote: 'Jewish criminal law knew four methods of execution: stoning, burning, decapitation and strangling (Mishnah, *Sanhedrin*, 7:1). It was customary to hang the bodies of executed blasphemers and idolaters on a stake (cf. Deut. 21:23 and Gal. 3:13: "A hanged man is accursed by God"). This, however, was merely to make the punishment more of a deterrent. When the Hasmonian King Alexander Jannaeus took vengeance on his political opponents and had them executed in gruesome ways, the author of a commentary on Nahum at Qumran remarked: "He hanged men alive, something that had never before happened in Israel".'

than the obvious implication that, however suitable an end this might be to a Jewish pretender to some sort of throne, it certainly did not enhance the spiritual claims made either by him himself, or by others on his behalf. And for Christians falsely to have attributed such a shameful death to their Lord and Master would be nothing short of incredible.

From the climate of thought which prevails today it is easy to underestimate this last point. The cross has become such a symbol of heroic self-sacrifice, and such a focal point of religious devotion, that it is difficult to realize how it must have appeared in the days of the early church. The closest modern parallel would be a gallows and a hangman's noose. There was nothing either romantic or mystical about crucifixion in the Roman Empire. It was an all too common form of execution, which not only provided a sickening sight of human agony, but also a rude reminder of the rule of an alien power. To die such a death would seem to show that the condemned man was a failure, a criminal, an object of pity or shame, repudiated by both God and men. No wonder the apostle Paul says that the preaching of the cross was to the Jews a stumbling-block, or cause of offence, and to the Greeks an absurdity (1 Corinthians 1:23). What possible motive could there have been for the primitive church to invent such an end to what they certainly believed was a life of matchless quality and supreme significance, or to accept the form of a cross as the central symbol of their faith and devotion?

The crucifixion, however, does seem to provide convincing proof of one point about which New Testament scholars have been much divided – and to which passing reference has already been made: namely, that Jesus himself *did* believe that he was the Messiah. It is true that he did not make any such claim explicitly in his public preaching – partly, no doubt, for political reasons, but largely because of the mistaken expectations this would have aroused among his hearers. But it was clearly as a potential threat to Rome that Pilate and his minions delivered him to a death largely reserved for 'the armed robber and the political insurgent' (Betz, p.84). This is explicit in the inscription on the cross: 'JESUS OF NAZARETH, THE KING OF THE JEWS' (John 19:19), which would seem to echo the Evangelists' report that part of the conversation between Pilate and Jesus had been about this very point (Matthew 27:11; Mark 15:2; Luke 23:3; John 18:33–37). And this, in its turn, must have been prompted by the fact that the 'blasphemy' for which the Sanhedrin had condemned him was his reply to the question (put to him on oath by the high priest), 'Are you the Christ, the Son of the Blessed One?' with the words: 'I am . . . . And you will see the Son of Man sitting at the right hand of the Mighty One and coming on the clouds of heaven' (Mark 14:61–64) – an affirmation that had naturally been reported by the chief priests to Pilate in explicitly political terms.

The only people I know of who deny that Jesus was crucified are Muslims, who base their denial on the Quranic verse: 'The Jews say "We killed the Messiah, Jesus, son of Mary, the apostle of God," though they did not kill him, and did not crucify him, but he was counterfeited for them [or 'it was made to appear to them that they did so'] . . . . But God raised him up to himself . . . .' This verse is taken by the vast majority of orthodox Muslims to mean that, when the Jewish leaders were about to have Jesus crucified, God could not allow that to happen to his chosen messenger, so he caught him up to heaven and cast his likeness on someone else – possibly Judas Iscariot – who was crucified by mistake in his place.

It is possible that this idea owes its orgin to the Docetic [2] assertion that only a simulacrum of Jesus was crucified; or it may, perhaps, have been suggested by the claim of some Gnostic sects that the 'aeon Christ' descended on the man Jesus at his baptism, but left him before the passion. On the first hypothesis Jesus would not have been crucified at all; on the second the man Jesus was crucified, but not the aeon Christ. But the most probable explanation is that Muhammad could not (and would not) believe that God would not somehow have intervened to save and vindicate a prophet.

---

[2] Docetism was one of the earliest Christian heresies (*cf*. 1 John 4:2–3; 2 John 7). Docetists believed firmly in the deity of Jesus, but denied his full humanity. He *seemed* to be a man, in the manner of a theophany rather than one who shared our nature.

## But did Jesus *die* on the cross?

Let us take it as certain, then, that Jesus was crucified. But is it equally certain that he actually died on the cross? It has not infrequently been argued that he did not. This theory was first propounded, so far as I know, by K. H. G. Venturini at the end of the eighteenth century. According to this view Jesus was certainly nailed to the cross, but he did not really die on the cross. What happened was that pain and loss of blood caused him to swoon and appear to be dead. Do not the Gospels themselves record that Pilate was surprised that he was 'already dead' (Mark 15:44)? Medical knowledge was not very advanced at that time; so he was taken down from the cross and laid in the tomb in the mistaken belief that life was extinct. Then the cool restfulness of Joseph's sepulchre so far revived him that he was eventually able to emerge from the grave; but his ignorant disciples could not accept this as a mere resuscitation, and proclaimed it as a resurrection from the dead.

Such is the theory in bare outline. It has been elaborated in recent years by a heretical sect of Muslims called the Aḥmadīya, who assert that the resuscitated Jesus first spent some time recovering his strength and conversing with his disciples in Jerusalem and Galilee; then headed northwards and met the apostle Paul when the latter was travelling from Jerusalem to Damascus; went on as far as north India to take his message to the 'lost sheep of the house of Israel' in the form of a tribe called the 'Beni Isra'il'; and finally died and was buried in Srinagar in Kashmir, where the tomb of an unknown sheikh has now been 'identified' as his burial-place. But none of this is supported by any valid evidence whatever.[3] I have recently had occasion to correspond on this subject with a scholar whose expertise in the languages, beliefs and customs of this part of the world is of international repute; and he informs me that there is no

[3]*Pace* J. D. Shams, *Where did Jesus die?* I obtained a copy of this curious book, written by a former 'Imam of the London Mosque', from Sierra Leone. After some quotations and assertions of very doubtful value, several attacks on the Gospels, and a description of how 'Paul and his collaborators' perverted what the author believes to have been the simple message of Jesus into the Christian faith as he sees it today (an amalgam of pagan misconceptions rather than the fulfilment of Old Testament prophecies and symbols referred to by Jesus himself), Shams quotes a number of statements likening the Afghans, Kashmiris and the 'Beni Israel of

trace of any ancient tradition there which would give credence to this story – in spite of the fact that wholly different religious traditions abound in that environment. Yet this strange theory is proclaimed by the Aḥmadīya not merely as a matter of faith but of almost demonstrable fact. Curiously enough, moreover, another imaginative variation of Venturini's theory has been propounded comparatively recently by Hugh Schonfield in an extraordinary book entitled *The Passover Plot*.

The first objection to Venturini's original suggestion, or its subsequent development by the Aḥmadīya, is that the Fourth Gospel is emphatic that steps were taken to make certain that Jesus was dead; for that, surely, must have been the reason for the spear-thrust in his side (John 19:31– 34). But even if, for argument's sake, it is postulated that his life *might* not have been wholly extinct, is it really likely that to lie for hours in a rock-hewn tomb in Jerusalem at Easter, when it can be distinctly cold at night, would so far have revived him, instead of proving the inevitable end to his flickering life, that he would have been able to loose himself from yards of grave-clothes weighted by pounds of spices, roll away a stone which three women felt incapable of tackling (Mark 16:1–3), and then walk miles on wounded feet?

But it was the sceptic, D. F. Strauss, who, as it seems to me, finally exploded this theory when he wrote:

> It is impossible that a being who had stolen half dead out of the sepulchre, who crept about weak and ill, wanting medical treatment, who required bandaging, strengthening and indulgence...could have given to the disciples the impression that he was a Conqueror over death and the grave, the Prince of Life, an impression which lay at the bottom of their future ministry. Such a resuscitation...could by no possibility have changed

Bombay' to the Jews, and suggesting an influx of the 'Ten Lost Tribes' to these parts (*pace* the 'British Israel' movement). This is followed by some theories about alleged similarities between Buddhism and Christianity. Finally, the author attempts to substantiate the 'discovery' (by the 'Promised Messiah' of the Aḥmadīya) that Jesus died and was buried in Srinagar – an attempt in which the assurance of the 'substantiation' seems only to be exceeded by the paucity of the alleged evidence. It should perhaps be added that most orthodox Muslims regard the Qadiani branch of the Aḥmadīya as 'apostates'.

their sorrow into enthusiasm, have elevated their reverence into worship (Strauss, Vol. I, p.412).

Nor could the disciples ever have made such a mistake
unless Christ himself had deliberately exploited their
credulity.

The new slant given to this theory in *The Passover Plot* is
equally unconvincing. Hugh Schonfield is correct, in my
opinion, when he insists that the Jesus of the Gospels is
explicable only on the basis that he was profoundly convinced that he was the promised Messiah, and that he
understood his Messiahship in terms of the suffering
Servant of the later chapters of Isaiah. But Schonfield then
goes so far as to suggest that Jesus decided that he must
stage what would appear to be a sacrificial death in accordance with Old Testament types and predictions, although
he hoped he might in fact survive. So he carefully concealed
this plan from the apostles, and revealed it only to
Nicodemus and one or two unknown friends in Jerusalem;
he deliberately provoked Judas into betraying him; he
arranged for one of those whom I suppose we must call his
fellow-conspirators to be ready near the cross with a
spongeful of some narcotic to dull his pain and induce
unconsciousness; and he planned that Nicodemus and his
friends should then take his seemingly lifeless body and
nurse it back to health and strength. In the event, however,
this plan was thwarted by the spear-thrust in his side. All
the same, Schonfield surmises that he may have been
revived for a very short time, during which he asked that
certain messages might be given to the apostles, before he
finally succumbed and was quietly buried. But none of this
was known to the apostles, who sincerely believed that he
had died on the cross; and they then, we are asked to
believe, mistook the unknown person who tried to bring
them Jesus' dying message – or, conceivably, a series of
different persons – for the Master they had known so well,
and fell into the error of thinking that he had risen from the
dead. This seemed to them confirmed by the fact that the
tomb was empty.

This is ingenious to a degree. The book is marked
throughout, however, by a willingness to stress the merest

detail in the Gospel records where this assists the writer's strange hypothesis, and to reject everything, however important, which points the other way. The possibility that the central figure might have been more than a mere man is not regarded as even worthy of consideration. Instead, he is made to act in such a way as to be guilty of leading those who were the chief recipients of his teaching sadly astray. Nor is there any suggestion as to why the unknown messenger was mistaken for Jesus himself, why the conspirators never told the apostles what had really happened, or what, indeed, would have been the outcome of this fantastic plot if it had succeeded.

A more recent book, *The Anastasis: The Resurrection of Jesus as an Historical Event*, by J. Duncan M. Derrett, has elaborated a still more ingenious, but wildly speculative, variety of the 'swoon' theory. He suggests that Jesus suffered 'clinical' or inchoate death on the cross, revived in the tomb, and was able to 'commission' his apostles before 'brain' death supervened. They then (probably at his instigation) cremated his body. (For those who want more details of this erudite but most unconvincing book to which I have only just had access, see the Appendix, pp. 158ff.)

## Why was Jesus crucified?

None of these suggestions is at all convincing, and there seems to be no doubt whatever that Jesus did in fact die on the cross. But why was it that he *had* to die? Can this be adequately explained in terms of the impact that his teaching and actions might be expected to have had on the Jewish and Roman authorities, and the reactions they were likely to provoke? Why was it that both Sadducees and Pharisees seem to have joined in an unnatural alliance to destroy him, and that the Procurator acceded – most unwillingly, it seems – to their demands?

On the basis of the picture of Jesus drawn by many Liberal Protestant writers, it is certainly difficult to understand why the Sanhedrin should have gone so far as to condemn him to death. The ethical ideals represented by the Sermon on the Mount might well provoke ridicule and even opposition, but would scarcely suggest that the one who taught them was so dangerous that he must be destroyed. It is true that he had challenged a form of religion which was largely concerned with the outward and ritual, and had taught that it was the inward attitude of the heart which really mattered; that he had often disregarded the 'traditions of the elders' and even denounced them as contrary to the Scriptures which they claimed to amplify; and that he had repeatedly pricked the bubble of Jewish exclusiveness. These things were enough to explain fierce hostility, but they would not adequately account for this strange combination of both Sadducees and Pharisees in demanding nothing less than his execution.

An examination of the New Testament records reveals that a number of different charges were brought against him at his trial. Basic to them all, however, seem to have been his assent when charged on oath to say whether he was the Messiah. On this point we can certainly agree with Hugh Schonfield; and it is easy to see how a claim to be the Messiah, as that term was then interpreted by the Jewish leaders, would naturally be represented as a claim to be a King when he was arraigned before the Roman Procurator. It was such a charge alone which would have overcome the strong repugnance which Pilate seems to have had to condemn him to death; for a claim to be another King would constitute a direct challenge to the Emperor. As Otto Betz puts it:

> it is clear from the very fact of crucifixion that Jesus was executed as a political insurgent according to Roman law. In the inscription on the cross the verdict is explicit: Jesus of Nazareth was 'the King of the Jews'. Since the Roman emperor had to be acknowledged as the lord of Judaea, a 'King of the Jews' was bound to be condemned as a rebel (or 'robber') and crucified. There can be no doubt that here the Gospel account is giving the unvarnished historical facts. For what stamps Jesus as a common criminal according to Roman justice cannot be ascribed to any apologetic or dogmatic viewpoint, particularly if Mark wrote his Gospel in Rome (Betz, p.84).

This would also explain the decision of the Sadducees that he must be destroyed, for they were primarily concerned with maintaining the political integrity of their nation and with safeguarding their own position. But it is much more difficult, at first sight, to understand why this should have provoked the Pharisees, who made up a significant part of the Sanhedrin, to an equally insistent demand for his death. This can, I think, be explained only by the further charge that he was guilty of blasphemy – a charge which would make the death penalty appropriate under Jewish law. And this, in its turn, means that he must have claimed (whether explicitly or implicitly) to be more than Messiah, as that term was then understood by the Jewish leaders. As C. H. Dodd put it:

> The evangelists, I conclude ... take the view that Jesus was charged with blasphemy because he spoke and acted in ways which implied that he stood in a special relation with God, so that his words carried divine authority and his actions were instinct with divine power. Unless this could be believed, the implied claim was an affront to the deepest religious sentiments of his people, a profanation of sanctities; and this, I suggest, is what the charge of 'blasphemy' really stands for, rather than any definable statutory offence.... Whether or not Jesus had put himself forward as Messiah, the implied claim was messianic at least, perhaps rather messianic plus ('The Historical Problem of the Death of Jesus', p.99).

Dodd's explanation of what he terms 'messianic plus' in the implied claims of Jesus is that he had spoken and acted 'in ways which implied that he stood in a special relation with God, so that his words carried divine authority and his actions were instinct with divine power'. This, as we have seen, is certainly true of the ministry of Jesus, and would no doubt be regarded by the chief priest as 'blasphemy' in the broad (rather than strictly statutory) sense of that term – as it was, indeed, by Jesus' hearers on a number of occasions (*cf.* Mark 2:7; Luke 5:21; John 10:33). But Betz connects it specifically, in the context of Jesus' trial (Mark 14:64), with Nathan's prophecy to David recorded in

2 Samuel 7 – on the basis of a 'fragmentary Qumran text'[4] in which this passage is 'applied to the Messiah and the godly of the end time'. I quote Betz's exegesis of 2 Samuel 7:

> In this prophecy David, who is considering building a temple, is taught by the prophet that God is in need of no such house. He will rather himself establish a place for his people (7:10) and make a house for the king (7:11). What is meant is the house or dynasty of David. God will 'raise' one of the king's sons and establish his kingdom for ever (7:12). God will be his father and he shall be God's son (7:14).... This Davidic king shall build a house for the name of God (7:13), i.e. the temple (Betz, pp.88f.).

This last clause in the prophecy had its literal and almost immediate fulfilment, of course, in Solomon. But it is clear from the words addressed by Zechariah to Joshua son of Jehozadak (in Zechariah 6:12–13) that, in the spiritual and long-term sense, Nathan's prophecy was basically Messianic: 'Tell him this is what the LORD Almighty says: "Here is the man whose name is the Branch, and he will branch out from his place and build the temple of the LORD ... and he will be clothed with majesty and will sit and rule on his throne."' It may well be that this is why Jesus is reported as having said: 'Destroy this temple, and I will raise it again in three days' (John 2:19).[5] This was, of course, one of the accusations brought against him at his trial by false witnesses; but in this instance the falsity of their testimony was limited to the fact that they alleged that his statement had begun with the words: 'I will destroy this man-made temple...' (Mark 14:58) – just as the false witnesses against Stephen subsequently alleged that 'we have heard him say that this Jesus of Nazareth will destroy this place and change the customs Moses handed down to us' (Acts 6:14).

[4]One of the 'Dead Sea Scrolls' (*cf. New Bible Dictionary*, pp.271ff. and 1004f.).

[5]Betz comments that 'the fact that Jesus actually spoke the words about the building of the temple will hardly be seriously doubted. Six passages in the New Testament testify to it, and if the saying sometimes seems obscure, that rather speaks in favour of its authenticity'. He adds that the objection that none of the disciples may have been a witness of the preliminary night 'trial' by some members of the Sanhedrin is valid, but that the two points reported by Mark – Jesus' saying about the temple and his claim to be the Messiah – 'immediately became public', as the taunts thrown at Jesus during the crucifixion show (Betz, p.91, with 87f.).

John explicitly records that 'the temple he had spoken of was his body', and he adds: 'After he was raised from the dead, his disciples recalled what he had said. Then they believed the Scripture and the words that Jesus had spoken' (John 2:21–22). But at the time when the words were spoken any prediction of his resurrection fell on deaf ears, since it seems never to have occurred to the disciples, during his earthly ministry, that Jesus would die a violent death, in spite of the fact that he had repeatedly spoken of suffering to come. Far from regarding the Roman gibbet at that time as inevitable, it in fact took them completely by surprise – as did also the resurrection.

## Why was his death seen in retrospect as inevitable?

It was not, in point of fact, because of the reaction of either the chief priests or the Roman governor that the disciples, even in retrospect, came to regard the Roman gibbet as 'inevitable' – for they certainly believed that Christ had gone to that death voluntarily. Had he not said to Peter in the Garden, 'Do you think I cannot call on my Father, and he will at once put at my disposal more than twelve legions of angels? But how then would the Scriptures be fulfilled that say it must happen in this way? (Matthew 26:53–54). It was only after the shattering experience of that agonizing felon's death, the bewilderment and blank despair that followed, and the almost unbelievable joy of the resurrection, that they began really to understand. It was on Easter Day itself that Jesus joined the two disconsolate disciples walking to Emmaus, asked them why they were so sad, and then said: 'How foolish you are, and how slow of heart to believe all that the prophets have spoken! Did not the Christ *have to* suffer these things and then enter his glory?' And then, Luke tells us, 'beginning with Moses and all the Prophets, he explained to them what was said in all the Scriptures concerning himself' (Luke 24:25–27. My italics).

Somewhat later the same evening he appeared to 'the Eleven and those with them' and repeated much the same teaching: 'This is what I told you while I was still with you,' he said (little though they had understood it at the time); 'Everything must be fulfilled that is written about me in the

Law of Moses, the Prophets and the Psalms.' Then he opened their minds so that they could understand the Scriptures. He told them, 'This is what is written: The Christ will suffer and rise from the dead on the third day, and repentance and forgiveness of sins will be preached in his name to all nations, beginning at Jerusalem. You are witnesses of these things' (Luke 24:44–48). It was only a few weeks, moreover, before Peter was bringing together the two sides of what had happened – the human and the divine – when he told the assembled Jews on the day of Pentecost: 'This man, who was put into your power by the deliberate intention and foreknowledge of God, you took and had crucified by men outside the Law' (Acts 2:23, JB). So the basic 'inevitability' of that death lay within the eternal purpose of God;[6] but the moral responsibility was that of the Jews, of the Romans, and of us all.

It is obvious, then, that the apostles regarded the crucifixion as something much more than a martyr's death, inflicted on its victim against his will. On the contrary, the early church clearly believed that the inevitability of the cross came from the will and purpose of Jesus himself, as well as Jewish malignity and Roman connivance. After all, he had taught that men should love even their enemies; that they should not resist those who sought to do them harm; that they should be willing to 'lose' their lives in order to 'save' them – and everyone knows that example is much more potent and persuasive than precept, and that actions speak louder than words. It was in a sense essential, therefore, that he should not only live as an example to others, but also die as their supreme example. 'Greater love has no-one than this,' he himself said, 'that one lay down his life for his friends' (John 15:13). Nor did this example go unheeded, for the apostles subsequently taught that 'Christ suffered for you, leaving you an example, that you should follow in his steps' (1 Peter 2:21), and that 'It is by this that we know what love is: that Christ laid down his life for us. And we in our turn are bound to lay down our lives for our brothers' (1 John 3:16, NEB).

All this is perfectly true so far as it goes, but it does not go nearly far enough. In their understanding of the meaning

[6]*Cf.* A. M. Ramsey, *God, Christ and the World*, p.89.

of the cross men are seldom in error in what they assert, but often in what, at least implicitly, they deny. It is true that it was almost inevitable, on a purely human level, that Jesus would meet a martyr's death; and it is also true that he no doubt felt constrained to go willingly to such a death as an example to mankind. But the New Testament writers do not attribute the inevitability of the cross exclusively to the machinations of his enemies or to the desire of Jesus himself to put his ethics into practice. On the contrary, the teaching of the early church gives a primary emphasis to what I shall call the Godward, rather than the manward, aspect of the cross. And it is equally certain that they depicted Jesus himself as voluntarily going to his death for a much more fundamental purpose than to provide a living – or dying – example of his ethical teaching.

If we are to take the Gospels at all seriously, it is inescapable that Jesus himself regarded the cross as inevitable, not primarily because of the hostility of the Jewish leaders, nor because he wanted to set a supreme example of self-sacrificing love and patient endurance, but because this was his Father's will and an essential part of his mission. Hugh Schonfield is certainly right, as I see it, when he insists that the Jesus of the Gospels was utterly convinced not only that he was the Messiah, but also that this must be interpreted primarily in terms of the 'Suffering Servant' of the later chapters in Isaiah.[7] Vincent Taylor, in three consecutive books on the atonement,[8] has come to precisely the same conclusion, and has emphasized the supreme place occupied by Isaiah 53 in the way in which Jesus himself interpreted his mission.

## The divine necessity for the cross

One of the most striking features in the Gospel records is the divine imperative which seems continually to have prompted Jesus' words and actions. Right from the time when, at the age of twelve, we read that he gently rebuked Mary and Joseph with the words, 'Didn't you know I had to

[7]*Pace* C. K. Barrett, Morna Hooker, *et al.* Cf. my *The Teaching of Jesus*, pp.162ff. The 'Servant Songs' can be found in Isaiah 42:1–4; 49:1–6; 50:4–9; and, with a special emphasis on 'suffering', in 52:13 – 53:12.

[8]*Cf.* Bibliography, p.168, below.

be in my Father's house?' (Luke 2:49), this divine imperative seems to have dominated his life. 'I must preach the
good news of the kingdom of God to the other towns also,
because that is why I was sent' (Luke 4:43), he said early in
his ministry. And as soon as Peter confessed, at Caesarea
Philippi, that Jesus was the Christ, he began to teach his
incredulous and unwilling disciples that 'the Son of Man
must suffer' (Mark 8:31). With increasing frequency, moreover, we find this divine imperative identified with, and
based on, the fulfilment of the Old Testament scriptures.
'The Son of Man is going the way appointed for him in the
Scriptures' (Mark 14:21, NEB) was one way in which he
referred to what he knew lay before him; and he went on:
'You will all fall from your faith; for it stands written: "I will
strike the shepherd down and the sheep will be scattered"'
(Mark 14:27, NEB). It is abundantly clear that his life was
lived, more and more, under the shadow of the cross. 'The
scripture *must* be fulfilled,' he said on a number of different
occasions; and on the very road to Gethsemane he quoted
from Isaiah 53 and said: 'For I tell you that this scripture
must be fulfilled in me, "And he was reckoned with trans-
gressors"' (Luke 22:37, RSV). So it is not surprising that the
risen Christ summed it all up by asking: 'Was it not
necessary that the Christ should suffer...?' (Luke 24:26,
RSV).

## Interpretations

But why, we may ask, was the cross so essential from the
point of view, not of men, but of God? To this several
different answers have been given – all of them correct in
their fundamental assertions, however misleading they
may be in their denials or implications. This is particularly
true of the answer we shall consider first, which may be
termed the subjective or humanistic view of the atonement.

### a. The subjective or 'humanistic' interpretation

This approach, which is commonly associated with Abelard
(AD 1079–1142), a younger contemporary of Anselm of
Canterbury, explains the purpose of the death of Christ on
the cross solely in terms of the change it was to bring about

in the hearts of men and women. Abelard's major emphasis was that the cross represents the supreme demonstration of God's love for sinful men. Naturally enough, this interpretation was welcomed by many theologians at the time of the 'Enlightenment', and it is still widely taught and believed today. Sometimes (as, we shall see, is also true of the other interpretations) it has been expressed in very extreme terms. But it is best understood, I think, if we summarize it in a way which is as close as possible to the teaching of the New Testament.

By nature we all love our own way; so we rebel against God and resent his demands on our lives and consciences. As a result, there exists what can be described only as a state of enmity (conscious or unconscious) between us and God, and we stand in desperate need of what the New Testament calls 'reconciliation'. But the Greek word for reconciliation not only conveys the sense of making peace and bringing together persons who were previously alienated from each other, but also of a change of heart which is effected in one or both of them. Who, then, the argument goes, needed this change of heart? Here both reason and the New Testament seem to answer that this was primarily true of men rather than of God. 'God is love', we read; 'God so loved the world that he gave his one and only Son'; 'This is love: not that we loved God, but that he loved us' (1 John 4:8; John 3:16; 1 John 4:10). It is man who rebels and resents; so it is man whose heart needs to be changed. And at first sight this seems to be the primary sense in which the New Testament speaks of God's work of reconciliation. It was at the cross that God supremely 'demonstrates [or 'commends'] his own love for us in this: While we were still sinners, Christ died for us' (Romans 5:8). 'From first to last this has been the work of God,' Paul wrote to the Corinthians. 'He has reconciled us men to himself through Christ, and he has enlisted us in this service of reconciliation. What I mean is, that God was in Christ reconciling the world to himself, no longer holding men's misdeeds against them, and that he has entrusted us with the message of reconciliation. We come therefore as Christ's ambassadors. It is as if God were appealing to you through us: in Christ's name, we implore you, be reconciled to God!' (2 Corinthians 5:18–20, NEB).

We shall note, later, that this is by no means the only side of the atonement, and clear indications of the other side can be discerned also in the New Testament use of the term 'reconciliation'. But according to the 'subjective' view the *primary* emphasis is that men are reconciled to God by the change of heart which he effects in them. How, then, does he do this? The answer is that he does it by and through the cross. For men, as we have seen, love themselves and their own way, and hate God and his demands – so they have a very inadequate view of the meaning and effects of sin. But when they come to see how evil sin is in the sight of a holy God – so black that even he could deal with it only at the cross; and when they realize that the God who must always hate sin yet infinitely loves the sinner – so much so that he was willing to go, in the person of Christ, all the way to an agonizing and shameful death; *then* they experience a change of heart, and begin to hate themselves and their sin, and to 'love, because he first loved us' (1 John 4:19).

Now all this is perfectly true, and it is, indeed, an important aspect of the atonement. It is quite unnecessary to distort this emphasis by remarking, as Hastings Rashdall does of Abelard, that 'he sees that God can only be supposed to forgive by making the sinner better, and thereby removing any demand for punishment' (Rashdall, p.359). As Abelard himself put it: 'To us it appears that we are none the less justified in the blood of Christ and reconciled to God by this singular grace exhibited to us in that His Son took our nature, and in it took upon Himself to instruct us alike by word and example even unto death, (and so) bound us to Himself by love; so that, kindled by so great a benefit of divine grace, charity should not be afraid to endure anything for His sake' (*cf.* Rashdall, p.359). In other words, as he states elsewhere, it is man's grief for sin which makes him *'fit* to be saved' (my italics).

Such a distortion of New Testament teaching would accord well enough with the paramount emphasis put today on the reformative motive in punishment; but the basic idea in the subjective interpretation of the cross may more worthily be expressed by saying that God is always longing to forgive men's sins, and the problem he has to solve is

how to make man *receive* his forgiveness, since true forgiveness necessarily implies a new relation between two or
more persons. According to this view the fundamental
meaning of the atonement is that God, our loving heavenly
Father, always suffers when his children sin, but we are too
hardened and rebellious to believe this or to let it affect our
attitude and conduct. So he came in the person of his Son to
die a death which constituted the supreme demonstration
of his love, thus making clear in time and human history
what had always been true in the eternal and transcendent
world. It is only when we come to understand this, even
dimly, that our rebellion is silenced and our pride abased;
and we are ready, at last, humbly to accept the forgiveness
which God has always been waiting to bestow.

As we have seen, this view has a firm basis in the New
Testament itself. Every time we sing that well-loved hymn
'When I survey the wondrous cross' we are giving expression to it (*cf.* Morris, p.61); for the emphasis, throughout
the whole hymn, is on the subjective effect which a
contemplation of the love and suffering of the cross effects
in our cold and selfish hearts. But it does not follow from
this that the meaning of the cross is exclusively, or even
primarily, subjective and that there was no objective
necessity for it which is at least equally – or even more –
fundamental. On the contrary, the biblical evidence for an
interpretation of the atonement which is not confined to its
effect on the hearts of men and women, but which involves
a radical transformation in the situation in which they find
themselves – a transformation which could be accomplished
in no other way – seems to me overwhelming.

When we try to determine in what, precisely, this
objective necessity for the cross consists we again find
ourselves faced with a division of opinion – or at least of
emphasis – between what Gustaf Aulén terms the 'dramatic'
or 'classical' view of the atonement, on the one hand, and
the 'juridical' or 'Latin' view, on the other (Aulén, pp.20ff.).
The first of these finds considerable support in the early
Fathers, quite apart from the New Testament; while the
second is usually traced back to Anselm of Canterbury,
although it, too, has a very firm basis in the Bible. Both

interpretations have at times been grossly exaggerated, and even caricatured; but both, in essence, express truths without which no interpretation of the atonement would be adequate.

## b. The 'classical' or 'dramatic' interpretation

The 'classical' view sees the meaning of the cross chiefly in a victory which God himself won in Christ over hostile powers – Satan, sin, death and hell. Some of the early Fathers took this idea to the most extravagant lengths. They argued not only that men by their sin had come under the power of Satan, but that he had actually acquired 'rights' over them; and they did not hesitate to assert that when Jesus said that he had come to 'give his life as a ransom for many' (Mark 10:45), that ransom was paid to Satan to set his captives free. Some of them even pictured God as making a bargain with Satan, offering to let him have Christ if he would release the souls of believers. But then, as Leon Morris puts it,

> Satan found that he had over-reached himself. He could get Christ down to hell when the Father handed him over, but he could not keep him there. On the first Easter Day Christ rose triumphant. He burst the bonds of hell and broke free. He returned to heaven whence he came and Satan was left lamenting. He had lost the souls he gave up in exchange for Christ, and he had lost Christ too' (Morris, pp.65f.).

Nor were the Fathers who propounded this view in the least disconcerted by the fact that this supposed transaction with Satan looks suspiciously like trickery and deception. On the contrary, they glorified in the fact that God

> could out-scheme Satan, as well as defeat him in a test of strength. One of the greatest of the early theologians, Gregory of Nyssa, likened the process of salvation to a fishing expedition. The deity of Christ was the fish-hook and his flesh the bait. Satan took the bait and was destroyed like any poor fish. And even Augustine of Hippo, surely one of the profoundest intellects of all time,

improved on this only by substituting a mouse-trap for a fish-hook! (Morris, p.66).

The extravagance of such views, however, should not obscure the truth that the New Testament itself declares that at the cross a victory was in fact won over Satan and the powers of darkness. It was by his death, the writer of the Epistle to the Hebrews asserts, that Christ destroyed 'him who has the power of death, that is, the devil' and delivered 'those who through fear of death were subject to lifelong bondage' (Hebrews 2:14–15, RSV). And it was at the cross, Paul says, that Christ 'disarmed the principalities and powers and made a public example of them, triumphing over them' (Colossians 2:15, RSV). There is no need to press the imagery to the extent of asking to whom the ransom price was paid, and the New Testament never does this. Metaphors should not be interpreted in such a literal way. But the fact remains that the victory was won, that Satan's captives were set free, that sin was 'put away' and that death and hell were vanquished. If God is God and if God is love, it was essential that this victory should be won; and it could be won only at the cross. Hence the inevitability of the Roman gibbet. But Christ *did* die and rise again, and Paul could exclaim, 'O Death, where is your victory? O Death, where is your sting? The sting of death is sin, and sin gains its power from the law; but, God be praised, he gives us the victory through our Lord Jesus Christ' (1 Corinthians 15:55–57, NEB). It is this aspect of the cross, as Aulén reminds us, which has always inspired the triumphant exultation of our Easter hymns.

The reason why this view does not appeal to the modern mind is not primarily the crude imagery in which some of the Fathers depicted it. It is partly because many people today question the very existence of a personal Devil, and partly because they regard any idea of God winning a victory over sin, death and hell as involving a form of dualism. But Aulén rightly insists that there is all the difference in the world between 'the absolute Dualism between Good and Evil typical of the Zoroastrian and Manichean teaching, in which Evil is treated as an eternal principle opposed to Good', and the scriptural concept of 'the opposition between God and that which in His own created world resists His will; between the Divine Love and the rebellion of created wills against Him. This Dualism is an altogether radical opposition, but it is not an absolute Dualism; for in the scriptural view evil has not an eternal existence' (Aulén, pp.20f.,n.).

It is noteworthy, in passing, how vividly the Fourth Gospel speaks of Christ being not merely grieved but positively angry or 'enraged' at the tomb of Lazarus; and this anger was not caused by his sisters' failure in faith or the unrestrained wailing of their guests, but rather by the ugly phenomenon of death itself. For death itself – or death as we now know it – would have had no place in a perfect world. On the contrary, death as corruption and decay, and hell as the embodiment of spiritual death, are both the result of rebellion and sin; and the God who loves the sinner necessarily hates both sin and its dire results. 'The spectacle of the distress of Mary and her companions enraged Jesus,' in the words of B. B. Warfield, 'because it brought poignantly home to his consciousness the evil of death, its unnaturalness, its "violent tyranny" as Calvin phrases it. In Mary's grief he contemplates – still to adopt Calvin's words – "the general misery of the whole human race" and burns with rage against the oppressor of men' (Warfield, pp.116f.). Nor is this divine antipathy lessened by the fact that both death and hell are judgments passed by God himself on the sin of which they are the inevitable outcome.

This apparent ambivalence is vividly illustrated by the attitude of Martin Luther (*cf.* Aulén, pp.67, 82ff.) – and, indeed, of a number of passages in the New Testament – to the 'Law'. It was God's law, and therefore essentially 'holy and just and good'; yet the apostle could write that 'sin gains its power from the law' (1 Corinthians 15:56, NEB), and that 'those who rely on obedience to the law are under a curse' (Galatians 3:10, NEB). So man had to be 'discharged from the law' (Romans 7:6, RSV), and 'redeemed . . . from the curse of the law' (Galatians 3:13, RSV), in the sense of a way of legal righteousness which he could never attain and which even provoked the very sins it forbade (Romans 7:7–11). So regarded, the law was itself one of the enemies from which Christ delivered us.

We find this interpretation of the cross, I think, much easier to understand if, instead of viewing it as a trial of strength between God and Satan (whom God *could*, at any moment, have destroyed, and will in fact finally condemn in his own good time) – or, indeed, as a battle between God and an almost personified concept of Sin, the Law, Death and Hell – we look at it from the point of view of how God has set us free. 'The Son of God appeared', John tells us, 'to destroy the devil's work' (1 John 3:8) – and thus, in patristic language, to deliver his captives. Satan had no 'rights' over us, but he had acquired power over us. So in the incarnation the Son of God became the Son of man. He shared our nature, learnt obedience in the school of suffering, and was 'tempted in every way, just as we are, apart from sin' (Hebrews 2:11; 5:8; 4:15). Then, on the cross, he took upon himself the judgment of the law we had so signally failed to keep, and 'in his own person he carried our sins to [or 'on'] the gallows' (1 Peter 2:24, NEB) – so there is now 'no condemnation for those who are united with Christ Jesus' (Romans 8:1, NEB). Finally, in his resurrection and ascension, he became the High Priest who can understand our every weakness, the Mediator of the New Covenant in which we receive a new heart and mind, and the Saviour who can save 'to the uttermost' because he is the pioneer, and will be the perfecter, of our faith (Hebrews 4:15; 8:6–12; 7:25; 12:2). This is the victory he won – and it could not have been won in any other way.

## c. The 'juridical' or 'Latin' interpretation

What Aulén calls the 'juridical' or 'Latin' view, on the other hand, finds the primary necessity for the atonement in the character of God himself. God is infinitely loving, but he is also holy and just; and the infinitude of his love for the sinner is itself the measure of his antipathy to the sin which constitutes an inevitable barrier between the sinner and himself. This is expressed in the New Testament in terms of the righteous judgment of God on sin and his 'wrath' against it – a wrath which is utterly different from the petulance which so often characterizes human anger, and which, far from being inconsistent with his love, is in fact its obverse side. Sin, the Bible teaches, is 'sinful beyond measure' (Romans 7:13, RSV); and the God who is himself the moral order of the universe cannot ignore it or act as though it did not exist. He longs to forgive the sinner, but this can be done only on a moral basis. First, sin must be shown in its real light, judged and condemned; only then can forgiveness be glad and free.

It will be objected by some, no doubt, that this is to go back to the retributive theory of punishment rather than to concentrate – as many advocate today – exclusively on its reformative and deterrent purposes. But this represents a shallow and inadequate attitude to the whole problem of crime and penology. To reform criminals, if this can be done, and to restore happiness and equilibrium to those whose crimes can often be traced to inward frustration, misery and despair, are obviously of vital importance; and we have already seen how the cross, when properly understood, is uniquely able to transform frustration into peace, misery into happiness, and despair into devotion. Nor would anyone deny the importance of the deterrent element in punishment. But both the reformative and deterrent purposes in punishment would lack any adequate moral basis were there not also a retributive element – the conviction that the criminal *deserves* such treatment, that his crime merits it, and that there is a necessary connection between the degree of his guilt and the severity of the penalty he must bear.

If we concentrate on the reformative purposes alone, the criminal who is truly sorry for what he has done should never be punished at all, however heinous his crime, and the criminal who is so hardened as to be beyond reformation should equally escape any penalty whatever. If, on the other hand, we stress the deterrent element alone, then severe punishment might often be imposed for a comparatively trivial misdeed, while all penalties should properly be discarded as utterly useless in some of those major crimes in which they are most unlikely to have the desired effect. This, however, would outrage the moral conscience. Even in everyday life it would be dangerous in the extreme to allow would-be reformers to take whatever action they believed to be best calculated to effect the necessary change in a social misfit, or to allow free rein to the motive of deterrence, without the essential moral criterion that men and women must not be treated contrary to their deserts or to fundamental considerations of justice. The trouble is that it is impossible for a human judge to know all the relevant facts – heredity, environment, temperament, circumstances and temptation – on which any completely just assessment of guilt must be based. None of these considerations, however, applies to God. He knows everything, and he can and does judge with absolute justice and understanding. But on that basis which of us could ever lift up our heads?

The problem, then, is obvious. God is love, and he longs to reconcile and forgive the sinner. But God is also 'light', or absolute moral holiness, and he cannot ignore the fact of sin. Sin must be judged, expiated or punished. There was only one way in which this problem – and the resulting tension, if we may so speak, in the very character and nature of God – could be resolved. God himself came in the person of his Son to live in the world he had made and to experience the frustrations and temptations inherent in human nature; and God in Christ identified himself with our sin and bore its penalty and consequences. So now he can be seen to be just and righteous, and to have vindicated the moral order, when he pardons and justifies the repentant sinner.

It is, of course, as easy to caricature this view of the inevitability of the cross, as we saw to be true of the 'dramatic' or classical view. It has in fact often been so caricatured, not only by its opponents but by those who most passionately proclaim it. Not infrequently it has been represented in terms of a stern and angry God being placated by a kind and loving Christ; or in terms of God visiting the sins of the guilty on the only *man* who was 'good enough to pay the price of sin'. Both perversions of the doctrine must be repudiated. The New Testament teaching about the 'propitiation' – for that is the word which, above all others, sums up what we are now trying to understand – does not carry the idea of sinful men seeking to appease a vengeful deity. On the contrary, the New Testament asserts that 'Herein is love,' – love at its very highest and best – 'not that we loved God, but that he loved us, and sent his Son to be the propitiation for our sins' (1 John 4:10, AV). It was not we who provided the propitiation, but he; and it was his incomparable love for the sinner which prompted him to do it. Nor was it Christ, apart from God, who provided it; it was God in Christ who planned and accomplished it. But the propitiation was necessary, none the less.

Inevitably, this can be described as a 'juridical' view. The Bible speaks repeatedly of God as the Judge of men, of sin as not only breaking our fellowship with him but deserving his righteous judgment and condemnation, and of the wonder of his grace in 'justifying' – or declaring 'not guilty' – the repentant sinner. But the juridical aspect, though inescapable, must not be exaggerated. The idea, so prominent in the Middle Ages, that the cross completed a juridical 'satisfaction' for sin, which the sinner could not adequately make for himself, is a dangerous distortion. This view, in its extreme form, insisted on man undergoing penances for his sins and trying to atone for them by works of supererogation, but emphasized that neither the one nor the other could ever 'satisfy' a holy God. So God himself, in Christ, provided an all-sufficient penance for sin, and an incomparable life of undeviating obedience, which made up for every human deficiency.

The teaching of the Bible, however, is far more radical than this. Any picture of the day of judgment which depicts it in terms of a giant pair of scales, with our sins on one side and our good deeds on the other, and with the righteousness of Christ thrown into the balance in our favour, is a pernicious perversion. The Bible teaches that a single sin is enough to separate us from God (James 2:10). Our salvation can never in any measure be from ourselves. It is the work of God alone, who by his free, unmerited favour declares sinners to be 'not guilty', free of the law, because he has himself, in the person of Christ, dealt with our guilt when he 'bore our sins in his body on the gallows' (1 Peter 2:24). So sin is not only forgiven but forgotten.

The question is often asked whether Christ died as our 'representative' or as our 'substitute'. If we use this language the answer must surely be that he was both. The essence of the atonement is that he was 'made like his brothers in every respect', made genuinely man. It was as such that he was not only 'tempted [or 'tested'] in all points just as we are', but went through the most horrific test of all on our behalf. So he was certainly our 'representative' – something that, as God, he could never be. But as man he could never have died *'in our place'*; for it would be gross injustice for an innocent man to be allowed to bear the penalty of the guilty. As the prophet Ezekiel taught long ago, *no* man can bear another man's sins (Ezekiel 18:4, 20). Only the One who made us, who put us in this world knowing what would happen, and who will be our judge at the great Assize, could do that. So it is only because Christ was both God and man that we can discern in his death both a 'substitutionary' and a 'representative' element.

It is important to emphasize in this context that the New Testament teaching about reconciliation puts an unequivocal emphasis on something that has been done by God to alter the position on his side as well as on ours. We saw that, in 2 Corinthians 5, the major emphasis is on man's need for a change of heart. But in the other great passage about reconciliation, Romans 5:1–11, the emphasis is on God's side. It was not, of course, that God needed a radical change of *heart* – from enmity to love – for, unlike man, he was always basically loving. But there was certainly a need for what we may, perhaps, term a change of *attitude*. As H. Maldwyn Hughes puts it:

> What the Atonement achieves is a change in the relation of persons, and no such change can be brought to pass without both parties being affected. Reconciliation is necessarily twofold... when God reconciles us to Himself, our relation to Him, and His relation to us are both set on a new basis (Hughes, pp.20f.).

On God's side the fundamental change was that sin had now been judged and condemned, so forgiveness could be glad and free. This is clear from the fact that even in 2 Corinthians 5 Paul bases his entreaty to us to be reconciled to God on the fact that God had made Christ 'to be sin [or 'a sin-offering'] for us' and no longer held our misdeeds against us (verses 21 and 19b). But it is much more prominent in Romans 5. Here 'peace with God' was effected by Christ (v.1), who 'died for the ungodly' (v.6). So now we are 'acquitted' by his atoning death (v.9), which saves us from God's righteous judgment on our sin (v.10). This reconciliation, moreover, is something we 'receive' as a gift (v.11). As P. T. Forsyth insists:

> Reconciliation was finished in Christ's death. Paul did not preach a gradual reconciliation. He preached what the old divines used to call the finished work.... He preached something done once for all – a reconciliation which is the base of every soul's reconcilement, not an invitation only (Forsyth, p.90.)

Human similes about divine realities are always dangerous, but to me the best simile here is that of an amnesty. In this a just and benevolent king finds it possible to issue a full and free amnesty to his rebellious subjects, by means of which the enmity between them – acute, but not of his making – can be put away. So now the rebels are invited, and even implored, to avail themselves of his offer, to lay down their arms, to return to a glad allegiance and to reciprocate his love.

## Conclusion

The church has always been of one mind in asserting that the cross is at the very heart of its faith and message, but there have been many different views, as we have seen, as to *how* it saves men from sin. One reason for this, as Leon Morris says, is the complexity of the subject.

> Sin can be regarded from many aspects. It is at one and the same time a transgressing of God's law, a debt, an incurring of guilt, a coming under the power of evil, and much more. Obviously anything that is able to deal effectively with all the aspects of all the sins of all men will itself be exceedingly complex. We must not expect it to be so simple that a child can understand it all. And when a thing is necessarily complex there is bound to be

a certain amount of disagreement as to what it means essentially (Morris, pp.58f.).

Properly viewed, however, the different ways in which the utter necessity for the cross has been explained are not contradictory but complementary. It is not a question of choosing one of these views to the exclusion of the others, but of seeing how the full truth necessarily includes them all.

The subjective view, as we have seen, is profoundly true, provided it is not taken in isolation. Man does, indeed, need a radical change of heart; he needs to begin to hate his sin instead of loving it, and to love God instead of hating him; he needs, in a word, to be reconciled to God. And the place, above all others, where this change takes place is at the foot of the cross, when he apprehends something of the hatred of God for sin and his indescribable love for the sinner.

The crucifixion would not really have demonstrated God's hatred of sin, however, had there been no need, on God's side, for the propitiation which alone makes it possible for him to forgive the sinner. Far from detracting from the cross as a demonstration of God's love, this gives it a validity and profundity it would otherwise lack. What would be the point of an empty display of love by a death which was utterly unnecessary except for its subjective appeal? It would be like a man saying he would throw himself into the sea and give his life to demonstrate the depth of his affection for someone standing safely on a pier. This might be love, but it would savour of lunacy. How different it would be, however, if he had plunged into the water to rescue a drowning man, and had succeeded in saving him at the cost of his own life. That would be true love – love in meaningful action – rather than hollow sentiment. So the love of God was demonstrated at the cross not by an empty show, but by his saving men from judgment and condemnation in the only way in which this could be done. And it was shown not primarily by the physical agony of crucifixion, but by the infinite spiritual cost of bearing the sin of the world.

Much the same line of argument also applies to the

'dramatic' or 'classical' view. It is certainly true that God won the victory at the cross over Satan, sin, death and hell, and that he set their captives free. But this was done not only by Christ 'tasting death for every man', but by his being 'made sin' for us and becoming the 'propitiation' for our sins. And the basic need for this propitiation could be only in the character of God himself.

How else can one explain the words of Isaiah 53, that 'he was wounded for our trangressions, he was bruised for our iniquities; upon him was the chastisement that made us whole, and with his stripes we are healed. All we like sheep have gone astray; we have turned every one to his own way; and the Lord has laid on him the iniquity of us all' (Isaiah 53:5–6)? How else can one understand the sacrificial system, and John the Baptist's identification of Christ as 'the Lamb of God, who takes away the sin of the world' (John 1:29)? In what other way can one explain Christ's own statement that 'this is my blood of the new covenant, which is poured out for many for the forgiveness of sins' (Matthew 26:28)? And how can one understand the agony in Gethsemane, except in terms of a ghastly shrinking, not primarily from the physical pain of crucifixion, but from bearing the world's sin? Or the awful cry of dereliction from the cross, except in terms of an agonizing experience of that severance of fellowship with God which is the basic and inevitable consequence of sin?

Of course we cannot explain *how* the Son, who was eternally of one substance with the Father, could experience this. That would be to plumb the innermost mystery of the Godhead, which is not given to mortal men. But that does not alter the revealed fact that this is what happened, and that he was in fact 'made sin' in our place. As Campbell Morgan put it:

> The logical, irresistible, irrevocable issue of sin is to be God-forsaken. Sin in its genesis was rebellion against God. Sin in its harvest is to be God-abandoned. Man sinned when he dethroned God and enthroned himself. He reaps the utter harvest of his sin when he has lost God altogether. That is the issue of all sin. It is the final penalty of sin, penalty not in the sense of a blow inflicted

on the sinner by God, but in the sense of a result following upon sin, from which God Himself cannot save the sinner. Sin is alienation from God by choice. Hell is the utter realisation of that chosen alienation. Sin therefore at last is the consciousness of the lack of God, and that God-forsaken condition is the penalty of the sin which forsakes God. Now listen solemnly, and from that Cross hear the cry, 'My God, My God, why hast Thou forsaken Me?' That is hell.... On that Cross He was made sin, and therein He passed to the uttermost limit of sin's outworking (Morgan, pp.215f.).

It is clear, then, that no examination of Christianity as a historical religion can fail to give the cross a central place. This in itself, however, is not enough; for we need to reckon not only with the fact that Christ died, but with the reasons why the Bible and the church join in asserting that this was both necessary and inevitable. That theologians should differ as to why, precisely, this was so is scarcely surprising. The great fact on which the New Testament insists, Leon Morris remarks,

is that the atonement is many-sided and therefore completely adequate for every need. Do we appear as guilty sinners deserving death? Our death penalty has been borne. Are we enslaved to sin? The price has been paid and we are redeemed. Are we unable to realize the greatness of the love of God? The cross reveals it as nothing else can. Do we need an example to show us which way to go? Christ gives us that example in His death (Morris, pp.80f.).

So we might go on, and it would be easy to conclude this subject with Morris's words: 'However we understand man's plight, the New Testament sees the cross as God's complete answer. Whatever needed to be done to put away our sin and to make us safe for eternity He has done. The atoning work is satisfying and complete' (Morris, pp.58f.). That is the explanation of the triumphant cry which echoes down the ages from that tortured figure on a Roman gibbet: 'It is finished!' (John 19:30). Yet even that is not complete without the resurrection and the ascended life of the once crucified Jesus, in which he is able to save his people not only from the guilt and penalty of sin, but 'completely'. So it is to the resurrection that we must now turn.

# 4
# The empty tomb: what really happened?

In this final chapter we come, inevitably, to consider what really happened on the first Easter morning. For the belief that Christ rose from the dead is not an optional extra of Christian theology, superimposed on his life and death to give a happy ending to what might otherwise be regarded as a tragedy of infinite beauty, overshadowed by doubts as to whether it was not, after all, a supreme example of magnificent defeat. On the contrary, it is the linchpin of each one of our previous studies.

## The credibility of Christian origins

In the first chapter, 'The historical basis: is it convincing?', we saw that one of our very earliest and best-attested pieces of evidence for the message proclaimed by the primitive church is the terse statement in 1 Corinthians 15 – almost credal in its form – that the apostolic tradition, at the very inception of the Christian faith, was 'that Christ died for our sins according to the Scriptures, that he was buried, [and] that he was raised on the third day according to the Scriptures' (1 Corinthians 15:3–4). We could be sure that this was not a tradition peculiar to Paul, but one shared and proclaimed by all the apostles (1 Corinthians 15:11).

It is significant, moreover, that Paul not only argues that, if Christ was not risen, then both his preaching and his readers' faith were without foundation, but also that the apostles themselves must be regarded as 'lying witnesses for God' (1 Corinthians 15:15, NEB). This was because their assertion of the fact of the resurrection had not been based on any *a priori* conviction that the Messiah must necessarily rise again (far from it!), nor on any subjective assurance that he had in fact done so. Rather, it had been based on a number of incidents in which one and another of them, or whole companies of them together, testified that they had actually seen the risen Christ and conversed with him. These conceivably 'mystical' experiences were, moreover, brought right down to earth by their conviction that the tomb was empty and that Christ's mutilated human body had not only disappeared but been transformed into a different sort of body. To this point we shall return later.

It seems, therefore, that the credibility of the whole apostolic testimony must stand or fall according to the view we take of the resurrection. We shall, of course, have to consider the possibility that those concerned were so mesmerized by a series of hallucinations, visions or psychological experiences of some sort, that they not only became convinced of their Master's spiritual survival, but felt compelled to interpret this in terms of a resurrection from the dead. It is precisely at this point that it will become imperative to assess the evidence for the allegation that the tomb was empty, and to consider whether this could not, anyway, be explained on some rationalistic basis.

Of one thing we can be sure; namely, that the proclamation of the resurrection lay at the heart of the apostolic preaching from the very first. The triumphant faith and witness of the first generation of Christians is evidenced by all the New Testament documents and even, however indirectly, by pagan and Jewish testimony – to say nothing of the strong circumstantial evidence provided by the growth of the primitive church. This faith and witness are inexplicable except on the basis of their conviction that the one whom they had come to accept as the promised Messiah, only to see their hopes dissolve into despair before the tragedy of the crucifixion, had in fact triumphed over death and the grave. But this, too, will demand more detailed consideration.

## The Person of Christ

The conclusion to which we come with regard to the resurrection is equally relevant – indeed, fundamental – to the subject of our second chapter, 'The central figure: how are we to regard him?' It is clear that Paul considered the resurrection to be the supreme proof of the deity of Christ, for he wrote that he had been 'declared Son of God by a mighty act in that he rose from the dead' (Romans 1:4, NEB). It was, moreover, a personal confrontation with the risen Christ which evoked from 'Thomas the doubter' the first full confession of Christian faith when he exclaimed, 'My Lord and my God!' (John 20:28), and which prompted the apostles as a whole to give him the worship which belongs to God alone. But why, it may be asked, should this be so? After all, other risings from the dead are recorded in both the Old and New Testaments, yet no-one has suggested that the persons so raised were in any sense divine.

To this two answers may be given. The first is that the resurrection of Christ is clearly distinguished, in the biblical records, from all those instances of men and women who were called back from death and the grave to a renewal of physical life, and who eventually had to die again. The risen Christ, Paul declared, *could* not die again; death no longer has any power over him (Romans 6:9). His risen body was no longer a 'natural' but a 'spiritual' body: immortal and imperishable (1 Corinthians 15:42ff.; *cf.* Philippians 3:21). The resurrection was not the resuscitation of a corpse, but a radical transformation (*cf.* Pannenberg, p.77).

113

Even this, however, would not be beyond the power of an omnipotent God. After all, it is to such a resurrection that all Christians look forward one day. So the true answer to the question why the resurrection was regarded by the early church – and should be regarded by us today – as the final proof of the deity of Christ must be found in the nature of the person he was and the claims he made during his life and ministry. As we saw in chapter 2, it is recorded that on a number of different occasions he foretold that he would not only be crucified but would rise again on the third day; and this, as Frank Morison powerfully argues in *Who Moved the Stone?*, is also the inescapable interpretation of his enigmatic declaration, 'Destroy this temple, and I will raise it again in three days' (John 2:19). This declaration formed an important element in the accusations brought against him at his trial before the Sanhedrin (Matthew 26:61; *cf.* also p.90, above). He even promised his bewildered disciples that, after he had risen from the dead, he would go before them into Galilee (Matthew 26:32). So it is clear that, if nothing had happened after their sad farewell to him on the cross or at the tomb, they (and certainly subsequent generations) would have concluded on reflection that he must have been mistaken and that his predictions could not be relied upon.

But even a foreknowledge and prediction that he would die and rise again, and a vindication of this prediction by its literal fulfilment, would not necessarily prove his deity. Some of his recorded assertions, however, went considerably further than this. He claimed on one occasion, as we have seen, not merely that God would raise him from the dead, but that he himself had power to lay down his life and power to take it again – and even that this action of his was, in some sense, the reason for his Father's love (John 10:17–18). And on another occasion he asserted that he was himself both the resurrection and the life (John 11:25).

But the point at issue is even more fundamental than that. As we saw in chapter 2, he frequently made claims which would have sounded outrageous and blasphemous to Jewish ears, even from the lips of the greatest of prophets. He said that he was in existence before Abraham and that he was 'lord' of the sabbath; he claimed to forgive sins; he frequently identified himself (in his work, his person and his glory) with the one he termed his heavenly Father; he accepted men's worship; and he said that he was to be the judge of men at the last day, when their eternal destiny would depend on their attitude to him. Then he died. It seems inescapable, therefore, that his resurrection must be interpreted as God's decisive vindication of these claims, while the alternative – the finality of the cross – would necessarily have implied the repudiation of his presumptuous and even blasphemous assertions.

## The Roman gibbet

Very similar considerations apply also to the subject of our third chapter, 'The Roman gibbet: was it inevitable?' Without the resurrection the natural interpretation of the cross would be a martyr's death, whether imposed upon him against his will by the malignity of his enemies or welcomed by him as the supreme opportunity to put his ethical teaching into practice. It might, I suppose, in *some* sense be regarded as a demonstration of the love of God, except for the fact that any convincing demonstration of God's *own* love must, surely, have involved a unique relationship between the one who died and the God whose love he was demonstrating. The so-called 'classical' view of the victory of the cross, however, would be meaningless on such a basis, for the shout of victory over Satan, sin, death and hell which rings through the New Testament and our Easter hymns is always associated with the dual message of Good Friday and Easter Day, with the cross *and* the resurrection, and would be empty and hollow if the Roman gibbet had not been followed by the empty tomb.

Even on the basically 'juridical' view of the meaning of the atonement, moreover, it is the resurrection which vindicates the efficacy of what Christ did on the cross. How else could we know that his sacrifice was accepted, that his death constituted our 'ransom' and that his blood was in fact the means and guarantee of the remission of our sins? It was with this thought in mind that Paul declared that Christ 'was put to death for our trespasses and raised for our justification' (Romans 4:25, RSV). He uses the term 'justification' here, not in the sense in which he usually employs it (namely, of the means by which sinful men and women are acquitted or accepted as righteous in the sight of a holy God), but rather in the sense in which we find it used in James 2 (namely, as the evidence and proof of that acceptance).

## An event of crucial importance

So the assertion of the primitive church, that Christ did in fact rise from the dead, is absolutely crucial to our whole subject, from beginning to end. Wolfhart Pannenberg, who himself considers the Gospel records of the life and teaching of Jesus as, in part, a projection into the past of the church's experience of the resurrection, regards the evidence for the resurrection itself as so convincing that he makes it the foundation-stone of his whole thesis (Pannenberg, pp. 108, 66ff., *etc.*). It is particularly noteworthy in this connection, moreover, that he is totally unimpressed by the argument which maintains that the proclamation of 1 Corinthians 15 is concerned only with the resurrection appearances, and knows nothing of an empty tomb – which was a later embellishment, found only in the Gospels. Whatever a Greek might have thought about a merely spiritual survival, he maintains, it would have been impossible for a Jew of the first century to write of Christ having died, having been buried and having been 'raised to life', if he thought of his body as still rotting in the tomb (Pannenberg, pp. 74ff.). And what would have been the point of adding the words 'on the third day' if he was thinking of no more than a spiritual survival (which must, inevitably, immediately follow physical death)?

It is totally inadequate to suggest, with Bultmann, that the resurrection is not an event which evidence attests, but rather a mythological way of proclaiming the saving significance of the cross – and that all the historian can affirm is the Easter faith of the disciples. On the contrary, the resurrection, as A. M. Ramsey insists, is

something which 'happened' a few days after the death of Jesus. The apostles became convinced that Jesus was

alive and that God had raised him to life. It is not histori-
cally scientific to say only that the apostles came to realize
the divine meaning of the Crucifixion for them or that
the person of Jesus now became contagious to them.
Something *happened* so as to vindicate for them the
meaning of the Cross, and to make the person of Jesus
contagious to them. The evidence for a stupendous
happening, which the New Testament writers mention,
was the survival of the Church, the appearances of Jesus
in a visible and audible impact on the apostles, and the
discovery that the tomb was empty. The several elements
in this threefold evidence no doubt had different degrees
of evidential weight for different people, and they have
such varying degrees still (Ramsey, *God, Christ and the
World*, p.78).

Beyond question there was a strong experiential or
existential element in the apostles' resurrection faith. Jesus
had been both their Master and friend, and they had firmly
'hoped that he was the one who was going to redeem Israel'
(Luke 24:21). But the crucifixion, as we have seen, took
them completely by surprise and shattered all their dreams.
To them a crucified Messiah simply did not make sense.
Instead of 'redeeming Israel', Jesus had been repudiated by
the Jews and executed by the Romans; and the very method
of his execution, while almost routine in such cases for the
Romans, was, in Jewish eyes, a sign of being 'accursed by
God'. It seems obvious, then, that it was not a return of
confidence in the significance of Jesus' life – or still less his
death – which brought his broken disciples to their Easter
faith, which they subsequently 'mythologized' in terms of
an empty tomb and a risen Lord. It was the solid fact of the
empty tomb and their totally unexpected encounters with
the risen Lord himself that brought them – although not
always at once – from despair to triumphant joy.

When the truth dawned it was 'existential' enough, in all
conscience. 'But there was always another side to the
process of belief.' To quote Michael Ramsey once more:

The apostles, for all the existential character of the Easter
faith, were yet at pains to confirm to themselves and to

others that it was a reasonable faith and that there were facts inexplicable apart from the Resurrection. There was not only the challenge of the existential encounter: there was also the challenge of evidence, the challenge to explain a number of events and experiences other than by the Resurrection. That was the significance of the catena of evidence cited by St Paul in 1 Corinthians 15, of the inclusion of the particular Easter stories within the tradition and of the collection of stories made by the evangelists. The Emmaus story illustrates the various ingredients in belief in the Resurrection. There was the climax, Jesus known and recognised in the breaking of the bread and vanishing from their sight: it was the moment of faith and encounter. But there had been previously the reflection on the divine purpose in the scriptures which the stranger had unfolded to them on the road. There had been the report that the tomb had been found empty, and that the discovery had been corroborated by other observers. There was the corroboration of the two disciples' seeing of Jesus at Emmaus by the news that the apostles in Jerusalem had also seen him.... To value these evidential facts is not, as Bultmann suggests, to lapse into a worldly-minded historicism, for the Easter faith, existential as it is, was and is related to evidential history. Christians believe in the Resurrection partly because a series of facts are unaccountable without it (Ramsey, *God, Christ and the World*, pp.79f.)

So we must now turn to this evidence and examine it – much in the way in which a historian weighs the evidence (documentary and circumstantial) for some event of the past, and a judge sums up and assesses the evidence (together with the arguments for and against it) put forward in a legal trial. But first we must, I think, pause to take note of a point which is continually emphasized by a number of theologians, particularly from the continent: namely, the nature of this 'crucial event'.

## Myth, 'proto-history', or a transcendent event firmly rooted in history?

It is often argued that the resurrection of Jesus should be thought of primarily in terms of the transcendental and revelational, rather than the basically historical, since 'the concept of "historicity" cannot grasp the essence of the resurrection witness, which *points rather to something which transcends history*' (Künneth, p.33. His italics) – somewhat, I suppose, like the creation and the incarnation. But in Künneth's case this is not because he has any sympathy with Bultmann's assertion that 'The Easter faith is not interested in the historical question', for he insists that the message of the resurrection of Jesus is 'passionately interested in the concrete and completed reality of the event – an attitude totally foreign to the mythical frame of mind'. This was why the resurrection of Jesus, when proclaimed in the centres of heathen religions,

> was not by any means felt to be a new, but fundamentally similar, myth: on the contrary, it was recognised and rejected in its offensive otherness . . . . The message of the resurrection did *not* appear to the contemporary world to be one of the customary cult legends, so that Jesus Christ would be a new cult hero standing harmoniously side by side with other cult heroes. But the message was in terms of strict exclusiveness: One alone is the Kyrios ('Lord'). Here every analogy fails. This witness, in contrast to the tolerance of the whole mythical world, comes with an intolerant claim to absoluteness which calls in question the validity and truth of all mythology (Künneth, pp.60ff.).

So Künneth insists that the church's witness to the resurrection 'was not interested in proclaiming a general religious truth in the symbolic language of myth, but in "actual experienced facts" . . . . Paul emphasises in regard to the "Easter history", according to G. Kittel, "that the fact of it is assuredly certified and that one can go and ask the eye-witnesses"' (Künneth, p.60). So it is to Paul's testimony that we must now turn.

## Paul's testimony

The earliest documentary testimony to the resurrection that has come down to us is in Paul's epistles, all of which abound in references to this pivotal point in the gospel he preached. Whether one takes the view that 1 Thessalonians, which was probably written from Corinth in AD 50, was the first of these letters, or whether one believes that Galatians was written from Syrian Antioch in AD 48 (immediately after Paul had received a report of the Judaizers' activities in Galatia, and just before the Council of Jerusalem) and therefore has an even better claim to be the earliest of his letters, both epistles include explicit references to the resurrection.

But we have already seen that it is in 1 Corinthians (commonly regarded, together with 2 Corinthians, Galatians and Romans, as Paul's 'capital' letters, which are attributed to him by virtually *every* reputable scholar) that the evidence is set forth in much the fullest detail. The composition of this letter is generally dated in AD 55 (although a margin of a year or two either way is possible); but the vital point is that it takes the evidence back some twenty years before that, since the apostle states in verse 3 of chapter 15 that he had already 'passed on' to the Corinthians 'first of all' (in priority of importance rather than time, it seems probable) the tradition he had himself received several years before.

Almost certainly he had 'received' this tradition in its essentials in Damascus, from Ananias and others, immediately after his own conversion – possibly within some two years, or little more, of the crucifixion. In any case he *must* have heard it in full, together with the names of the principal witnesses, on his visit to Jerusalem 'after [another] three years' (which *may* have been considerably less than three full years, since Jews would regard this phrase as including the end of one year, the whole of the next, and the beginning of the third). He pinpoints the time and purpose of this visit, with unusual insistence and solemnity, in Galatians 1:18–20. It was 'to get acquainted with Peter', with whom he stayed for two weeks ('fifteen days' by Jewish reckoning); and the only other 'apostle' he saw was 'James, the Lord's brother'.

There has been a good deal of argument about where, precisely, in 1 Corinthians 15 the original tradition ends and where Paul breaks into his own words. Some would put the dividing-line at the end of verse 4, others at verse 5, and yet others at verse 7. But this seems to me singularly unimportant; for, however this may be, he must have been told of the appearance to 'more than five hundred of the brothers at the same time' during his conversations with Peter, and of that to James probably from his own lips. So we have Paul's testimony to all this evidence – which was, he asserts, the common testimony of the apostolic band (v.11) – dating back to what Dodd terms 'almost certainly not more than seven years, possibly no more than four', after the crucifixion (Dodd, *Founder*, p.168).

What is clear is that the words 'most of whom are still living, though some have fallen asleep' (v.6) represent an insertion by Paul himself – and it would be difficult to find a more significant 'aside' anywhere in the New Testament. Paul was no fool, and he had many opponents. Yet in these words he put his whole credibility at stake; for what he wrote was, in effect, an implicit invitation to any who doubted his statement to put it to the test, since the majority of five hundred witnesses were still available to be questioned. And in the ancient world it would not have been a terribly difficult task to contact some of them.

We have in this passage, then, the explicit testimony of Paul to Peter's and James's accounts of their own encounters with the risen Lord, of that of 'the Twelve', of 'more than five hundred of the brothers at the same time', and of that to 'all the apostles' (or the apostolic band?). He received the accounts within some five years of the event, they were apparently confirmed by all the apostles (v.11), and he committed them to writing about twenty years later. To this he immediately adds his testimony to his own experience on the Damascus road some two or three years later than these encounters during the 'forty days' – an experience which he both equates with, and yet (as we shall see) differentiates from, the others. How, then, can this explicit testimony – 'not to any generalized Christian experience', but 'to a particular series of occurrences, unique in character, unrepeatable, and confined to a limited period' (except in the case of Paul himself) legitimately be called in question? (*Cf.* Dodd, *Founder*, p.168.) 'Anyone who, in spite of this, would doubt their reliability must', in Campenhausen's words, 'perforce doubt all the deliverances of the New Testament – and not stop there!' (Campenhausen, p.45).

The most radical riposte of all – that the stories of Easter and the succeeding forty days were mere lies or fabrications – must, I think, be decisively repudiated. Consider the number of the witnesses; the quality of the ethical teaching they gave to the world and which, even on the testimony of their detractors, they lived out in their lives; and the fact that none of them, whether under the pressure of sustained persecution or even a martyr's death, seems ever to have gone back on the testimony he had given. Consider, too, the psychological absurdity of the idea that a band of men should be transformed, almost overnight, from craven cowards huddled in an upper room into a company of witnesses whom no opposition could silence, by nothing more convincing than a miserable deception they had conspired to foist upon the world. A guilty secret of that sort is far more likely to turn boldness into cowardice than vice versa.

The idea that these stories might be regarded as legends rather than lies might, in the abstract, seem somewhat more plausible. Had it been possible to date the records a century or two later (and repeated attempts to deal with them in this way have, in fact, been made by a series of brilliant scholars), the suggestion might have been feasible. All such attempts, however, have decisively failed, crushed under a weight of contrary evidence; and there can be no reasonable doubt that the testimony to the resurrection can be traced back to the very first decade after the event. It seems meaningless, therefore, to speak of legends when we are dealing, not with stories handed down from generation to generation, but accounts given by the eyewitnesses themselves or attributed to them while they were still present to confirm or deny them.

Besides, who can read these stories with any care and then dismiss them as mere legends? It would have been a great temptation to a legend-monger to recount some story of how the resurrection happened; yet no such attempt finds a place in the New Testament. What legend-monger would ascribe the first interview with the risen Christ to Mary Magdalene, a woman of no great standing in the Christian church? Would he not have ascribed such an honour to Peter, the leading apostle; or to John, the 'disciple whom Jesus loved'; or – more likely still, perhaps – to Mary the mother of our Lord? And who can read the story of the appearance to Mary Magdalene, or the incident in which the risen Christ appeared to two disciples on Easter Day on an afternoon walk to Emmaus, or the episode in which Peter and John raced each other to the tomb, and seriously conclude that these are legends? They are far too dignified and restrained; far too true to life and psychology. The difference between them and the sort of stories recorded in the apocryphal Gospels of a century or two later is both striking and significant.

No; so far as I know there are no responsible critics today who suggest that these stories are either lies or merely legends. On the contrary, they admit – as admit they must – that the apostles firmly believed that their Master had risen from the dead; but they then proceed to suggest first that this belief, however sincere, was a subjective conviction rather than one based on adequate objective evidence, and then that a number of legendary accretions crept into the stories between the time of the Pauline testimony and the composition of the Gospel records. This second suggestion rests largely on the accounts of the 'empty tomb' – an item which, if true, itself provides *part* of the evidence that the disciples' convictions were based on an objective reality. So let us turn immediately to this point.

## The empty tomb

A number of suggestions have been made on this subject; but chief among them – at least in the context of legendary accretions which may have become attached to the original witness of Paul – is the assertion which is often made that Paul 'knew nothing of the empty tomb' to which he 'made no reference whatever', direct or indirect. But this is an idle assertion which is contradicted by the facts. It is, of course, perfectly true that he did not dwell on the point in 1 Corinthians 15, where his primary purpose was to prove – and, in part, explain – the resurrection to which Christians may look forward, rather than to provide details about the resurrection of Jesus. His references to the latter at the beginning of the chapter were to lead on to the question in verse 12, 'But if it is preached that Christ has been raised from the dead, how can some of you say that there is no resurrection of the dead?' – an argument reinforced, with various permutations, in the following verses. But it seems to me ridiculous to argue from this that Paul 'knew nothing of the empty tomb'. After all (as we have noted in passing), what Jew of the first century could possibly have written 'that Christ died for our sins' (physically, of course), 'that he was buried' (again, physically, of course), and 'that he was raised on the third day' (1 Corinthians 15:3–4) if he had believed that the body of the crucified Lord was still lying where it had originally been laid in the tomb?

The Greeks, it is true, had a vague belief in a shadowy survival of the spirits of the dead in an underworld, but this was not an understanding of the nature of man, or of the meaning of resurrection, which would have been recognized by Jews. Those Jews who believed in the resurrection at all understood it in a far more literal way – and that 'at the last day' (John 11:24), not in the middle of history. Yet the fact remains that, as Michael Ramsey puts it:

> The words of the tradition, as Paul reproduces it, seem incomprehensible unless they mean that the body of Jesus was raised up .... Died-buried-raised: the words are used very strangely unless they mean that what was buried was raised up .... In default of the strongest evidence that Paul meant something different and was using words in a most unusual way, the sentence must refer to a raising up of the body. The most radical of critics, Schmiedel, and the most scientific of critics, Lake, agreed that *belief* in the empty tomb is implied in the words (Ramsey, *The Resurrection*, pp.42f.).

In this context Dodd quotes a number of passages which 'can be traced back to a time well before the composition of the gospels', and then comments:

> It seems hard to resist the conclusion that this is how the early Christians, from the first, conceived the resurrection of their Lord. When they said 'He rose from the dead', they took it for granted that his body was no longer in the tomb; if the tomb had been visited it would have been found empty. The gospels supplement this by saying; it *was* visited, and it *was* found empty (Dodd, *Founder*, p.166).

They do indeed; this is the explicit, and sometimes detailed, record of all the four Gospels. A number of different women visited the tomb, found the stone rolled away, saw the empty space where the body had lain, were told by one or more angelic messengers that he had risen, and were given messages for his disciples. At Mary's instigation, moreover, both Peter and John visited the tomb and found that it was indeed empty (John 20:1–9).

Two further points should be added in confirmation of this fact. First, it is a matter of history that the apostles made a considerable number of converts in Jerusalem, within a very few weeks, by preaching the resurrection. To a Jewish audience, however, any mention of a resurrection, or God 'raising Jesus from the dead', would inevitably have suggested to their minds something to do with the tomb; and anyone could have walked to Joseph's tomb, from any quarter of Jerusalem in which they heard this proclamation, in under an hour. It is unbelievable that many did not do so – and that they did not find that the story was true. Paul Althaus put this bluntly when he wrote: 'In Jerusalem, the place of Jesus' execution and grave, it was proclaimed not long after his death that he had been raised. The situation *demands* that within the circle of the first community one had a reliable testimony for the fact that the grave had been found empty.' Then, with understandable hyperbole, he adds that the proclamation of the resurrection 'could not have been maintained in Jerusalem for a single day, for a single hour, if the emptiness of the tomb had not been established as a fact for all concerned' (*cf.* Pannenberg, p.100).

Secondly, Pannenberg himself states that

> Among the general historical arguments that speak for the trustworthiness of the report about the discovery of Jesus' empty tomb is, above all, the fact that the early Jewish polemic against the Christian message about Jesus' resurrection, traces of which have already been left in the Gospels, does not offer any suggestion that Jesus' grave had remained untouched. The Jewish polemic would have had to have every interest in the preservation of such a report. However, quite to the contrary, it shared the conviction with its Christian opponents that Jesus' grave was empty. It limited itself to explaining this fact in its own way, which was detrimental to the Christian message (Pannenberg, p.101).

## Rival hypotheses about the 'empty tomb'

Taking it for granted, then, that the body of Jesus could not be found, is there any satisfactory way in which this can be explained on purely natural grounds? A number of suggestions have in fact been made and demand at least a cursory examination. So to this we must now turn.

The earliest attempt to explain the phenomenon of the empty tomb in an eminently straightforward way is recorded in Matthew's Gospel, where we are told that the Jewish leaders bribed the guard (which had been set to watch the sepulchre) to report that the disciples had come by night and stolen the body (Matthew 28:11–15). But no-one, so far as I know, accepts this story today. It would be incredible both in ethics and psychology. Imagine the apostles raiding the tomb by night, stealing the body, burying it furtively in some other place, and then proceeding to foist this miserable deception upon the world. This would run totally contrary to all we know of them: their ethical teaching, the quality of their lives, their steadfastness in suffering and persecution. Nor would it begin to explain their dramatic transformation from dejected and dispirited escapists into witnesses whom no opposition could muzzle.

Better than this is the suggestion that the body might have been moved to another grave, for some reason or other, on the orders of the chief priests or the Roman Procurator, or even of Joseph of Arimathea. But we need to remember that in seven short weeks Jerusalem was seething with the apostles' preaching of the resurrection. They were proclaiming it up and down the city, to the great discomfiture of the chief priests, who were being accused of having conspired to crucify 'the Holy and Righteous One' (Acts 3:14) at the hands of an alien power – and were prepared to go to almost any lengths to stamp out this dangerous teaching.

Why, then, when the apostles started preaching the resurrection, did they not issue an official denial, and state that the body had been moved on their orders? If this would not have sufficed, they could have called as witnesses those who had carried it away. If this was not enough, they could have pointed to its final resting-place, or even produced the body itself. They could have exploded this disturbing heresy finally and decisively. Why, then, did they not do so? The answer seems inescapable: because they could not; because they did not themselves know where the body was. And exactly the same argument would apply to the Roman Procurator. The Romans, too, must have been considerably disturbed by this proclamation that a criminal so recently executed because he claimed to be a King, in apparent rivalry to the Emperor, had risen again from the dead. It is incredible that, if the body had been moved on their orders, they would not have told the chief priests and taken steps to crush this dangerous movement at its very beginning, by showing that the apostles' preaching was without foundation.

What, next, of Joseph of Arimathea? The answer is, I think, that the critics cannot have it both ways. They must either accept what the Gospels say, that he was a secret disciple; or they must suppose that he was a pious Jew, who agreed to bury the body in his own tomb so that it might not hang on the cross on the sabbath day. But if he was a Christian it is most unlikely that he would have moved the body without consulting the apostles first; and it is fantastic to suggest that he would not have told them afterwards, when they were preaching the resurrection up and down the city. Yet this would lead to the impossible hypothesis that the apostles themselves were blatant deceivers, preaching a miracle which they knew perfectly well had never happened. If, on the other hand, he was just a pious Jew, then it is unlikely that he would have moved the body without asking the permission of the chief priests, and incredible that he would not have told them afterwards, when they were so upset by this proclamation of the resurrection. But why, then, did they not annihilate this dangerous heresy at its very inception by issuing an official denial, by calling Joseph as a witness, or even by producing the body itself?

Another attempt to explain the phenomenon of the empty tomb was first advocated, I believe, by Kirsopp Lake in *The Historical Evidence for the Resurrection of Christ*. The women who saw where Christ was buried, we are reminded, were strangers in Jerusalem, and their eyes may have been blinded by tears. They went to the tomb, moreover, in the half-light of early morning. So they might have missed their way and gone to the wrong tomb. This, he suggests, was precisely what happened; and a young man, who chanced to be hanging around, guessed what they wanted. 'You are looking for Jesus... who was crucified,' he told them. 'He is not here' (pointing to the tomb at which they were looking). 'See the place where they laid him' (pointing to another tomb). But the women became frightened and ran away; and subsequently they decided that the young man must have been an angel who was proclaiming the resurrection of their Master from the dead.

This theory is most ingenious, but it scarcely stands up to investigation. To begin with, it is based on accepting the beginning and the end of what the young man said, but rejecting the most important part in the middle. For what the young man is recorded as having said was: 'You are looking for Jesus... who was crucified. *He has risen!* He is not here. See the place where they laid him' (Mark 16:6). This changes the whole meaning; and it seems strange for a scholar to mutilate the record in this way without any textual authority whatever. Even so, the theory does not seem to make much sense; for if the women had gone straight back to the apostles with this story, they would surely have done one of two things: either they would have gone to the tomb themselves to investigate what had happened, or they would have started to preach the resurrection at once. Yet all the records state that they did not do this for another seven weeks; and no Christian would have had any reason to invent this interval.

We are asked to believe, then, that the women did not, in fact, tell the apostles this story for some weeks, since the latter had all left Jerusalem post-haste for Galilee. (No doubt Galilee was a healthier spot for Christians just then, but we are not told why the apostles were so singularly ungallant as to run away and leave all their womenfolk behind – wives, sisters and mothers!) The women, it is suggested, remained alone in Jerusalem, for no apparent reason; and it was only some weeks later, when the apostles came back, already convinced by some psychological experiences that Jesus was still alive, that they told them this story – and the apostles then put two and two together and made seven or eight out of them and started preaching the resurrection. But on this hypothesis the body of Jesus would still have been lying in Joseph's tomb, about which the chief priests must have known or could so easily have made enquiries. So why did they not obliterate this dangerous movement by denying the very basis of the apostolic preaching, or even by displaying the decomposing body of the one whose resurrection was so confidently proclaimed?

## Some miscellaneous further hypotheses

The suggestion has also been made that the body might conceivably have been removed by some common despoiler of tombs. But why? No riches could have been anticipated from the grave or its contents, and a Jew of that period could scarcely be suspected of stealing bodies on behalf of anatomical research! The place where it was reburied, or even the bones or shroud of Jesus, might well have been exploited for purposes of pilgrimage, veneration, superstition or magic; but had this been the case some record would certainly have come down to us, since it would have been of the greatest interest to the Jewish authorities.

Again, it has been suggested that the body might have been disposed of in a common grave in which several criminals were buried, and even that its site had been forgotten. But this would involve falsifying so very much of the Gospels with a care and ingenuity which stagger the imagination – including, *inter alia*, the account of Joseph of Arimathea's request for the body, Pilate's surprise that Jesus should be dead already, Nicodemus's co-operation, and the women who watched the burial, to say nothing of all the subsequent visits to the tomb. Are all these passages not only to be regarded as fictions, but as supremely cunning inventions designed for this very end? Very soon, moreover, the chief priests (and, most probably, the Roman Governor) would have given a lot to be in a position to scotch the preaching of the resurrection, with all that this involved. So a common thief could expect a handsome reward, rather than any punishment, if he had produced the body.

As we have seen, another hypothesis is the 'swoon-theory': that Jesus was taken down from the cross in a state of complete collapse but not actually dead, that he subsequently revived, and that the tomb was empty because its occupant had never really died. But few of those who advocate this theory today can have read the caustic comments on the sceptic Strauss (see pp.85f., above). These comments were directed against the original theories of Venturini, Paulus and *possibly* Schleiermacher;[1] but the wholly unsubstantiated 'revelations' of the Aḥmadīya, and the fertile imagination of Hugh Schonfield in *The Passover Plot*, do nothing to support the suggestion (see pp.84–87, above). This theory would leave the apostles honest but quite unbelievably stupid; the little band of conspirators – including Jesus himself – as guilty tricksters; the object of the whole exercise nebulous to a degree; and the survival of the church (together with centuries of Christian experience) wholly unexplained.

[1] *Cf.* James Orr, *The Resurrection of Jesus*, pp.11, n.2, and 42, n.4; Milligan, p.76, n.2.

## Two final points about the tomb

It is also noteworthy in this context that all the explicit references to the empty tomb come in the Gospels, which were written for Christians who wanted to know the facts. In the public preaching to those who were not yet convinced, as recorded in the Acts of the Apostles, there was an insistent emphasis on the resurrection, but not a single reference to the tomb. For this I can see only one explanation. There was no point in speaking of the empty tomb, for everyone – friend and foe alike – knew that it was empty (*cf.* Pannenberg's statement about early Jewish apologetics on pp. 125f., above). The only points worth arguing about were *why* it was empty, and what its emptiness proved.

Yet in point of fact the tomb was not wholly empty. In one of the most vivid of all the stories about the first Easter morning we read how Peter and John, summoned by Mary Magdalene's news of the stone which had been rolled away from the entrance of the sepulchre, set out to investigate. Half-way along the road they broke into running; and John, the younger man, outran Peter and got there first. Stooping down, he peeped into the tomb and saw the grave-clothes; but, typically enough, he stayed outside, wondering. Soon after, Peter arrived and characteristically blundered straight in. He took note of 'the strips of linen lying there, as well as the burial cloth that had been around Jesus' head' – not lying with the linen strips, but apart, wrapped into one place. It was as though the body had withdrawn itself, leaving the strips of linen as they were, separated from the head-cloth by the space where Jesus' neck had been. As William Temple puts it (and I have in part followed his rendering of the Greek), 'It is extraordinarily vivid, and such as no invention would devise, no freak of imagination conjure up' (Temple, p.378). Peter does not seem to have seen the significance, and went home musing; but for John, who had followed him into the tomb, it was enough: 'he saw and believed' (John 20:1–8).

It is also significant that no suggestion has come down to us that the tomb became a place of reverence or pilgrimage in the days of the early church. Even if those who were convinced Christians might have been deflected from visiting the sepulchre by their assurance that their Master had risen from the dead, what of all those who had heard his teaching, and even known the miracle of his healing touch, without joining the Christian community? They, too, it would seem, knew that his body was not there, and must have concluded that a visit to the tomb would be pointless.

The second point is that, although explicit references to the empty tomb are confined to the Gospels, all four of them bear unequivocal witness to the fact that it was indeed empty. As Künneth puts it: 'this report is inseparably bound up with the message of the resurrection and as specific "Easter Gospel" is rooted in the faith of the primitive Church.... A message of the resurrection of Jesus without news of the empty tomb does not exist at all events in the tradition of the primitive Church, and is a theological abstraction' (Künneth, pp.91f.). It is true that attempts have been made, and are still being made, to eliminate the question of the empty tomb. But this rests, in my view, on a rationalistic approach which simply ignores the recorded facts. Künneth remarks that theologians such as Emile Brunner overstate when they assert 'the plain fact that Paul reckons his encounter with the Risen One, which is quite different from those depicted in the Gospels, to be identical with those of the original disciples' (Künneth, p.92. *Cf.* pp.134f., below).

Künneth himself, with all his scholarly caution, rightly insists that

it is extremely difficult to see how the Gospel accounts of the resurrection could arise in opposition to the original apostolic preaching and that of Paul.... The interest of the primitive Church surely centred solely on handing on the witness of the apostles as unspoiled as possible, and most especially the witness to the resurrection of Jesus which was of such decisive importance. Here the very details of the account were of priceless worth and invention by the Church contrary to the apostolic witness had no place among the Church's interests, nor could it have failed to be sharply contradicted by the apostles or their pupils. Must we not in face of these critical objections reckon precisely on the contrary with the possibility that the various pieces of witness are essentially the same in kind? Could it not be that Paul and the original apostles mean the same as the Gospel accounts, even when they do not tell the story so colourfully as the latter? The 'fact' of the difference is still unproven, or at least cannot be proved from the silence of the apostles.

It appears indeed to be as good as certain that the account of the empty tomb was definitely included in the apostolic tradition, and that it is therefore completely impossible to speak of any silence of the apostles on the matter. Paul asserts both that 'he died' and that 'he was buried', and expressly affirms his agreement with these statements. Hence according to the apostolic tradition the resurrection of Jesus can hardly have been thought of otherwise than as being raised from the tomb... (Künneth, pp.92f.).

Künneth also adds in a footnote (on p.94) that, in the light of K. Bornhäuser's detailed examination, the conclusions in regard to the resurrection of Jesus appear to be as follows: '1. The raising of Jesus can have been thought of by Paul and by the whole primitive Church only as a bodily one. 2. Consequently the conviction of the empty tomb of Jesus becomes as a matter of course an element in faith in the resurrection of Jesus. 3. The fact of the empty tomb as such, however, does not have any power to prove the resurrection ... so that Paul, too, like the rest of the New Testament, does not adduce the fact of the empty tomb as a specific argument.' In other words, the empty tomb is only one element in the total evidence.

## The resurrection appearances

There can, however, be no doubt that the principal thrust of the apostolic witness was to their encounters with the risen Christ, and it is to them that we must now turn. As we have just seen, Paul's testimony in 1 Corinthians 15:1–11 raises, *inter alia*, the question of the nature of those appearances – since he seems, at first sight, to put his own encounter with the risen Lord much on a par with the appearances during the 'forty days' reported in some detail in the Gospels. He describes it by precisely the same word (*ōphthē*, 'he was seen by') which he uses in regard to the appearances to Peter, to 'the Twelve', to the 'five hundred', to James and to 'all the apostles' (verses 5–7). Thus many scholars have concluded that Paul made no distinction between his experience on the Damascus Road and those that he had just mentioned. But the way in which he introduces his own testimony ('and last of all he appeared to me also, as to one abnormally born', verse 8), shows that he did regard his experience as somewhat different from theirs, for he makes it clear that the appearance to him 'was something unexpected, exceptional, and abnormal, an appendix to a series already closed' (Dodd, *Founder,* p.181, n.6). But the difference, I am convinced, was one of form and substance, as well as time and sequence.

It has been widely suggested, of course, that there are differences between the form of all the appearances of the risen Lord as these are described in the Gospels and as they are listed in Paul's testimony; and that 'while Paul witnesses to purely spiritual visions, they are represented as progressively more materialistic as the gospel tradition develops'. But John Robinson rightly insists that the only real evidence for this thesis ('namely, that a purely spiritual resurrection is more probable and therefore more primitive')

is that Paul regarded all the other appearances as conforming to the pattern of his own vision on the Damascus Road. But there is little basis for such a deduction. So far from regarding his own vision as normative, he marvels at his right to include it in the series at all. Paul, in fact, says nothing about the manner of the appearances, nor does he equate even his own seeing of the Lord (1 Cor. 9:1) with his other 'visions and revelations' (2 Cor. 12:1–7). In the gospel records it is arbitrary to arrange the appearances in order of increasing materialisation.... All the appearances, in fact, depict the same phenomenon, of a body identical yet changed, transcending the limitations of the flesh yet capable of manifesting itself within the order of the flesh (*Interpreter's Dictionary*, IV, pp.47f.).

So it seems to me that what Paul intended to emphasize in 1 Corinthians 15:8 was that his own encounter with the risen Lord was just as real and 'objective' as that of the other apostles, not that theirs were as 'visionary' as his. As Stephen Neill puts it, the word Paul uses of himself means 'something born *before the right time*'; and 'if we take this seriously, Paul can only mean that he has seen by anticipation the glory of Christ as that will be manifest in the Parousia' (Neill, *Interpretation*, p.287).

## Paul's testimony and the Gospel records

In point of fact critics have, in my opinion, made far too much of the differences between the appearances listed by Paul and the various encounters recorded in much more detail in the Gospels, on the one hand, and of the alleged discrepancies between the accounts given in the different Gospels, on the other. The fact that Paul starts his list with Peter, for example, and that he confines his named witnesses to men, does not imply that he did not know that the first appearance of all was to Mary Magdalene. It merely indicates that the basic tradition he cites concentrated particularly on apostles, and that it took account of the fact that in the ancient world the testimony of men was accorded greater weight than that of women.

It may seem strange that in the Gospels the special appearance to Peter is mentioned only (and then very briefly) in Luke 24:34. But it is distinctly possible that this interview – after Peter's threefold denial and bitter self-recrimination – was so intimate that Peter simply confirmed the women's report that the Lord was risen, kept all the details of this exceedingly personal experience to himself, and preferred to recount the conversation recorded in John 21:15–22 – underlined, as this may have been, by the special message to him given to the women at the tomb by the 'young man' in Mark 16:7 ('Go, tell his disciples and Peter, "He is going ahead of you into Galilee. There you will see him"').

The appearance to 'the Twelve' probably corresponds to that reported in some detail in Luke 24:36–48. On that occasion only ten of the apostles were actually present, but 'the Twelve' had become a generic term. Critics are apt to comment with surprise on the fact that those present were 'startled and frightened', in spite of the reports they had already heard from the women, Peter and the two from Emmaus. But surely there is nothing strange in this, seeing that the Lord appeared suddenly to a group most of whom had not yet seen him, who were meeting together in fear behind locked doors and who at first thought that he might be a ghost (*cf.* Luke 24:37). He reassured them partly by showing them 'his hands and side' and partly by asking them if they had anything for him to eat (John 20:20; Luke 24:39–43); for the marks of his suffering and death identified him as none other than their crucified Master, while the invitation, 'Touch me and see', together with the fact that he actually ate a piece of fish, proved that this was no phantom. Clearly the risen Lord did not *need* to eat. But nothing else could so readily have reassured them of his actual presence, put them at their ease, and brought home to them the sense that they were renewing the fellowship they had so often enjoyed with him as he had conversed and eaten with them in the past (*cf.* Acts 10:41). We will revert to this point, and to the nature of his risen body, again (see also p.113, above).

The encounter with 'five hundred of the brothers at the same time' may, or may not, refer to the appearance reported in Matthew 28:16. The fact that some of those present on that occasion still 'doubted' (verse 17) indicates that 'the eleven' were by no means the only participants. There is no report in the Gospels about the appearance to James; but the fact that this previously unbelieving 'brother of the Lord' subsequently became the leader of the Jerusalem church, and wrote about his human brother as 'our glorious Lord Jesus Christ' (James 2:1) can, no doubt, be traced to this interview. The appearance to 'all the apostles' could refer to that reported in John 20:26–29 (when Thomas, previously absent, was present), to that reported in John 21:1–22 or to some other incident to which the Gospels make no specific reference.

The appearance to Paul on the road to Damascus is reported three times in the book of Acts (9:1–7; 22:6–11 and 26:12–18). The assertion that these three references to the same inverview are mutually inconsistent is shallow in the extreme. In Acts 9:7 we are told that Paul's companions 'heard the sound but did not see anyone'; and in 22:9 that they 'saw the light, but they did not understand the voice of him who was speaking'. There is no contradiction here: they heard the *sound* of the voice, but did not understand what was said; they saw the *light* from heaven, but did not see the One from whom it shone. It was only Paul who both heard the actual words and saw the speaker. As for the differences in the records of what was said, it seems clear that, in the account Paul gave to Agrippa in Acts 26, he incorporated in what he heard on the Damascus Road – in the interests of brevity, no doubt – some of the information he had, on that occasion, been assured would be 'told him' in the city (*cf.* Acts 9:6; 22:10). After all, the message Ananias was commanded to give him was, in essence, part of the same revelation.

This is not the place to deal in any detail with the manifest differences, and alleged contradictions, between the records about the resurrection given in the different Gospels; and a very few words must suffice. I will turn first to the manifest differences. In Mark the original text apparently ends at 16:8, and we can only speculate as to whether the original ending got lost (and what it may have contained), or whether, possibly, the Gospel was intended to end with the account of the empty tomb and the angelic message. Matthew concentrates on the appearance in Galilee (and the 'Last Commission') recorded in 28:16–20; but the assertion that this Gospel includes *no* appearance in Jerusalem is manifestly mistaken, since the encounter with the women recorded in 28:8–10 must be located in Jerusalem.

Luke, by contrast, concentrates on Jerusalem; and critics are apt to say that he knew nothing of any appearances in Galilee, and even that he places all the appearances which he records on Easter Day itself. But this is absurd in the light of all the statements he makes in Acts 1:2–11, where we are told that Jesus appeared 'to the apostles he had chosen' over a period of 'forty days' – sometimes, no doubt, in Galilee – 'gave many convincing proofs that he was alive ... and spoke about the kingdom of God'. Then, 'on one occasion' (verse 4), he evidently told them to stay in Jerusalem, and to wait there 'for the gift my Father promised' – their baptism with the Holy Spirit. A careful study of Luke 24 reveals more than one place[2] where there was probably a break in what looks, at first sight, like a consecutive narrative (*cf.* Ramsey, *Resurrection*, p.66); and the compression of this final chapter in a very long Gospel may well be explained by the fact that his writing material (or papyrus) may have been running short. As for John, the assertion that chapter 21 – 'appendix' though, in some sense, it may be – is not 'authentic', seems to be purely arbitrary. So appearances both in Jerusalem and Galilee are recorded in some detail in this Gospel.

So much for the manifest differences in the Gospel records, and we shall not pause to discuss the speculations that have been made as to why Mark's Gospel may have been cut short, why Matthew was chiefly concerned with Galilee and Luke with Jerusalem, or why John's Gospel seems to come to a natural end and then to add a very valuable appendix before a further impressive conclusion. But what of the alleged discrepancies and contradictions in some of the recorded incidents? I have considered some of these, in a degree of detail, elsewhere[3]; so I must content myself here with a few desultory remarks.

First, it is important to realize in this context that these alleged discrepancies and contradictions may indeed, at least at first sight, constitute a problem for one whose primary preoccupation is the precise accuracy of the biblical records, but not for one whose immediate concern is the strength of the evidence for the resurrection. On the contrary, they make that evidence all the more convincing. For the fact is that honest witnesses, who have not conferred together or been 'coached', normally differ considerably in their testimony, particularly in matters of detail. Almost inevitably each of them sees the incident concerned from a somewhat different angle; each 'sees' – or comprehends – only part of what he could have seen; and each remembers only some of what he did in fact see. As a result their initial accounts will usually differ greatly, and may appear to be

[2] *E.g.* after 43 or 44 (or both), and 49.
[3] *A Lawyer among the Theologians*, pp.108–115, 119, 121–149, and *passim*.

somewhat contradictory. But it is common experience that, when they hear the evidence of other witnesses, this will remind them of memories in their subconscious minds that they had not consciously noted or recalled, or will make them see some fact or circumstance from another angle – with the result that their evidence proves to be supplementary rather than contradictory. Often, however, this will become clear only when one testimony is laid alongside another – or several others – and the witnesses concerned are asked whether the stories they first told were in fact incompatible with those told by their fellows.

Second, I must confess that I am appalled by the way in which some people – biblical scholars among them – are prepared to make the most categorical statements that this story cannot *possibly* be reconciled with that, or that such and such statements are *wholly* irreconcilable, when a little gentle questioning of the witnesses, were this possible, might well have cleared up the whole problem. Sometimes, indeed, a tentative solution may not be very far to seek even without such questioning, although the suggested reconciliation cannot, of course, be proved; and in others there may well be a perfectly satisfactory solution which evades us. I would refer any interested reader to a few examples of the sort of thing I have in mind in *A Lawyer among the Theologians* (chapter 4), or to *Easter Enigma* by John Wenham.

Third, it may be observed that, if the greater part of five hundred witnesses to the resurrection, including several of the apostles, were alive when 1 Corinthians was written in c.AD 55, a very considerable number of them must have been still living when our Gospels, in the Greek form which has come down to us, began to appear – and still more when the gospel tradition was taking shape. What is crystal clear, moreover, is that exceedingly little was done to reconcile the different traditions on this subject. Interplay of some sort there must have been; but each Evangelist tells the story of the resurrection as he is moved to tell it, and as best fits the total picture he feels constrained to present, with little or no concern to bring it into line with any parallel pictures. In spite of all that source, form and redaction criticism may disclose, there is a robust independence in the stories regarding the resurrection appearances, and the empty tomb with its attendant angels, which each Evangelist recounts.

## Hallucinations and similar phenomena

Mention of angels at the tomb reminds us that it is impossible to be dogmatic about the relative roles played by objective and subjective elements in such an experience as seeing angels. One man or woman may see an angel when another does not; but this does not prove that the angel had no objective reality. People who allege that they have seen angels may, indeed, be indulging in fantasy; but it is equally possible to postulate that a certain subjective awareness must be added to objective reality before an angel, who is normally invisible to human eyes, can be seen by men. In the context of the empty tomb, moreover, it is strange how reluctant some critics are even to allow that the angels concerned might appear and disappear, that they need not have stayed in one position, or that some visitors to the tomb might have been so awed by the supernatural as to see, remember or mention one angel who spoke to the exclusion of one who was present but remained silent.

We have already seen that, in the case of Paul's experience on the Damascus Road, the vision and message were seen and heard by Paul alone, although evidence of their 'objectivity' may be found in the sound and light which his companions heard and saw. Paul, so far as we know, had never met Jesus during his earthly life, so the risen Lord identified himself by answering Paul's wondering question 'Who are you, Lord?' by the words 'I am Jesus, whom you are persecuting' (Acts 9:5). But during the forty days when the risen Christ appeared, on a number of different occasions, not as a vision from heaven but almost as though he were resuming, very fleetingly, his terrestrial life, it is noteworthy that these appearances were confined to those who had known him, and that in each case they were able to recognize him – not, indeed, always at once, but eventually with conviction – by some special feature, action, gesture or tone of voice.

It may seem strange that the risen Christ was not always recognized instantaneously. In the case of Mary Magdalene, it seems clear that she scarcely looked, through her tears, at the face of the man she took to be 'the gardener', and it was only when Jesus addressed her as 'Mary', in the way she knew so well, that she immediately 'turned towards him and cried out in Aramaic, "Rabboni!"' (John 20:11–16). Several suggestions have been made as to why the two disciples walking to Emmaus 'were kept from recognizing him' for so long. But two important points must always be remembered.

First, that the earlier appearances were totally unexpected. The disciples had never understood that the one they had come to regard as the Messiah must suffer and die, in spite of his warnings; so they were wholly unprepared for the resurrection. It was not their residual faith that prompted them to express the significance of Christ's life and death in the 'mythological' terms of an empty tomb and a risen Lord, but their totally unexpected, and objective, encounters with him that transformed their dumb despair into triumphant faith.

Second, we have already seen that the risen Christ was no resuscitated corpse, but that his 'natural body' had been transmuted into a 'spiritual' or 'heavenly' body – and it could not have looked exactly the same.

But could the resurrection appearances possibly be explained in terms of individual or group hallucination of some sort – psychological experiences in which those concerned sincerely believed, but which need not necessarily have been founded on solid facts? We have already noted a number of factors which seem to point decisively against this conclusion. Let us pause, however, to consider the phenomenon of hallucinations as such, and see whether the resurrection appearances conform to the criteria which commonly characterize psychological experiences of this variety.

To begin with, such experiences seem to be almost exclusively confined to persons of certain distinct psychological types. But it is impossible to reduce all those who claimed to have seen the risen Christ to any such classification. There was a Mary Magdalene, who *may* have been an emotional, imaginative or highly-strung young woman. But there was also a hard-headed tax-collector, a 'doubting' Thomas, an ex-Zealot, and a number of down-to-earth fishermen. And what of the five hundred?

Again, experiences of this kind are highly individualistic, since they spring, in part at least, from the past experiences and subconscious minds of the persons concerned. One man's hallucinations, therefore, will almost certainly differ from another's. But here, we are told, five hundred people, on one occasion, had the very same 'hallucination' at the same time; while on other occasions ten, eleven, and seven individuals had precisely the same 'fantasy'. So it looks very much as though these experiences were based on objective facts rather than subjective impressions.

Such experiences, moreover, usually concern some expected event. A mother whose son runs away to sea, let us suppose, lights a lamp every evening in the confident hope that he will one day come home; and eventually she imagines that she sees him walking in at the door. But in this case the evidence is convincing that the apostles were not expecting any such thing. They *ought* to have been, since Christ had foretold his death and resurrection; but they had not even begun to understand what he was talking about. Instead, they were shattered, disillusioned, in despair.

Hallucinations and similar experiences also, I am told, normally occur at suitable times and in appropriate surroundings. But it is impossible to reduce the resurrection appearances to any such formula. There were two near the tomb early on Easter morning; one in the course of an afternoon walk into the country; another, on the same day, in the form of a personal interview, presumably in broad daylight; two or more in a room in the evening; one on a hill in Galilee, and another beside the lake; and yet another on the Mount of Olives.

Finally, hallucinations, if repeated at all, normally go on recurring over a very considerable period – either increasing in frequency until some crisis is reached, or decreasing in frequency until they die away. But in this case five hundred people claim to have had one such experience, and a number of people to have had several such experiences, all during a period of forty days. Then these 'hallucinations' abruptly ceased, and not one of the persons concerned ever claimed to have had another. True, Paul subsequently claimed to have had a vision of the risen Christ when he was on the road to Damascus, and John on the island of Patmos. But it is clear, I think, that these and other visions which people have claimed to have had down the ages – and which, in the case of Paul and John, I unhesitatingly accept as genuine – differed in substance from what happened during the forty days when the risen Christ went in and came out among his disciples in what they afterwards described as 'many infallible proofs' (Acts 1:3, AV).

Nor is it feasible, in my view, to explain the resurrection appearances in terms of the phenomena claimed by modern spiritism. I am no authority on this subject; but it is impossible to find any one medium present on all occasions, or even the usual group of seekers after the supernatural. And the one who appeared seems to have been very different from alleged spiritist emanations. He could be distinctly heard and clearly seen, even in broad daylight – although his resurrection body was different from his 'natural' body, and he was recognized only with some difficulty. He could withdraw from grave-clothes, leaving them, it would seem, still in place; he could pass through closed doors; he could appear and disappear; yet he could invite a finger to explore the mark of the nails in his hands, or the spear-wound in his side. And he could even eat a piece of broiled fish.

But should not this last point, at least, be regarded as a mythological addition to the true facts of the resurrection? Does it not betray a tendency to equate the resurrection with a return to natural life, with its need of food and sustenance? Some would, indeed, have it so. For myself, I am convinced that Christ's deathless spirit returned to his mutilated human body and that this was transformed into what Paul calls a 'spiritual' body (*cf.* 1 Corinthians 15:44). What that is like I frankly do not know; but there is so much else that we do not understand, living as we do in a world of three dimensions. This transformed body would certainly not have needed food; but that does not mean that the risen Christ *could* not have eaten, any more than that he *could* not be touched. And one reason for his request for food seems to me clear enough (see p.136, above). Had it not been for this, his disciples might have concluded, once his visible presence was withdrawn from the upper room, that they had merely seen a vision. But when they looked at the bones of the fish, or the plate on which it had lain, this interpretation of their experience would be impossible; they had objective proof that someone had really been there.

However this may be, it seems to me of fundamental importance to remember that the empty tomb and the resurrection appearances go together. It is easy to argue that all that really signifies is that the Christ of the Gospels is alive today, and that men can still come to know him. What does it matter, then, what happened to his body? In reply it must be emphasized that not only does the credibility of the apostolic witness stand or fall by the validity of their testimony on this point, but also that it is the empty tomb which decisively differentiates between the resurrection of Christ and any sort of ghost story. It is not only that Jesus is still spiritually alive and that his disciples somehow became aware of this; the evidence points to the fact that his 'natural' body was transformed into a 'spiritual' or celestial body (1 Corinthians 15:42–54) in which he left the tomb, 'showed himself alive after his passion by many infallible proofs' (Acts 1:3, AV), and ascended to heaven; so we now have a glorified Man on the throne of the universe.

## Circumstantial evidence

The documentary testimony to the resurrection is also supported by a great deal of circumstantial evidence. First, there is the existence of the Christian church. This institution can be traced back in history to Palestine early in the first century. But to what did it owe its origin? Its documents of association, as a lawyer might term them, state unequivocally that it owed its very inception to the resurrection of its founder from the dead. This was the fundamental conviction and message of the apostles and their entourage. 'From the very first', as C.F.D. Moule has reminded us, the conviction that Jesus had been raised from death has been that by which their very existence has stood or fallen. There was no other motive to account for them, to explain them . . . . At no point within the New Testament is there any evidence that the Christians stood for an original philosophy of life or an original ethic. Their sole function is to bear witness to what they claim as an event – the raising of Jesus from among the dead . . . . The one really distinctive thing for which the Christians stood was their declaration that Jesus had been raised from the dead according to God's design, and the consequent estimate of him as in a unique sense Son of God and representative man, and the resulting conception of the way to reconciliation (Moule, *Phenomenon*, pp.11, 14, 18).

It is not too much to say, with C. S. Lewis, that 'the Resurrection, and its consequences, were the "gospel", or good news which the Christians brought: what we call the "gospels", the narratives of Our Lord's life and death, were composed later for the benefit of those who had already accepted the *gospel*. They were in no sense the basis of Christianity: they were written for those already converted. The miracle of the Resurrection comes first' (Lewis, *Miracles*, pp.147f.).

Again, there is the phenomenon of the Christian Sunday. Almost all the first Christians were Jews, who shared the deep regard in which all their race held the *seventh* day of the week, as 'the Sabbath to the Lord [their] God' decreed as part of the covenant of Sinai. Jesus had, of course, demonstrated their freedom from petty, man-made regulations; but it seems that Jewish Christians continued, for some decades at least, to observe it as a day for rest and synagogue worship – although it was not imposed on Gentile Christians. But it is clear that from a *very* early date Christians, both Jews and Gentiles, began to meet together on the evening of the *first* day of the week to 'break bread' in celebration of the resurrection (Acts 20:7). It was for this reason that it soon became known as 'the Lord's Day' (Revelation 1:10) – and was imposed on all, under Constantine, to take the place of the Jewish Sabbath.[4]

[4]See D. A. Carson (ed.), *From Sabbath to Lord's Day*, pp.280f., 285–302.

There is also the festival of Easter, which occupies much the same place in history. But Easter would be utterly meaningless without the death and resurrection which it commemorates.

Then, too, there is that significant interval of seven weeks between the resurrection and its first public proclamation. As has already been observed, no Christian would have invented this. But how can it be explained – except on the basis of the Gospel records, which tell us that the apostles were absorbed, for the first forty days, in intermittent interviews with their risen Lord, and that they then waited a further ten days, on his instructions, until the Holy Spirit came upon them in power?

Far and away the strongest circumstantial evidence for the resurrection, however, can be found in the startling change in the apostles themselves, to which passing references have been made already. How can one explain the change in Peter, from a man who denied his Master three times before household servants, into one who told the chief priests to their face that God had raised from the dead the one whom they had crucified, and who then assured them that 'salvation is found in no-one else, for there is no other name under heaven given to men by which we must be saved' (Acts 4:12)? The New Testament tells us the secret. The broken-hearted Peter, with his self-confidence shattered, had a private interview with his risen Lord (Luke 24:34; 1 Corinthians 15:5), and later the Holy Spirit came upon him (Acts 2:1ff.; 4:8). What transformed James, Jesus' unbelieving brother throughout the years of his ministry, into the chairman or bishop of the Jerusalem church a few years later? The New Testament reveals this secret too, for we read that the risen Christ had a personal interview with James (1 Corinthians 15:7). This explains why he subsequently wrote about his human brother as 'the Lord of glory' (or 'our glorious Lord Jesus Christ', James 2:1).

As Pannenberg puts it: 'The Easter appearances are not to be explained from the Easter faith of the disciples, rather, conversely, the Easter faith of the disciples is to be explained from the appearances' (Pannenberg, p.96). And what of Paul? How can we account for the fact that the arch-persecutor of the Christian church so soon became its greatest missionary – except on the basis of his vision of Christ on the road to Damascus? And is it conceivable that such a man as he would not have checked up on the facts regarding Joseph's tomb, were it not that he must have known already that it was empty? What the vision of the risen Christ showed him in a flash was *why* the tomb was empty, and who its former occupant really was.

We have already noted, moreover, that Paul not only insisted that Christ 'died for our sins according to the Scriptures', but also that he 'was raised on the third day according to the Scriptures' (1 Corinthians 15:3–4). No doubt one of the predictions he had in mind was from Psalm 16, which reads:

> Therefore my heart is glad, and my soul rejoices;
>   my body also dwells secure.
> For thou dost not give me up to Sheol,
>   or let thy godly one see the Pit.
> Thou dost show me the path of life;
>   in thy presence is fullness of joy,
>   and in thy right hand are pleasures for evermore
>                     (Psalm 16:9–11, RSV; *cf.* Acts 2:25–28).

Another passage to which he would almost certainly have pointed is Psalm 110:1; for it is clear that Peter interpreted the words 'The LORD says to my Lord: "Sit at my right hand until I make your enemies a footstool for your feet"' (*cf.* Acts 2:33–36) in terms of the resurrection. And another obvious passage is the prediction in Isaiah 53, just after the most explicit references in the Old Testament to the vicarious nature of Christ's death and to some of the circumstances of his crucifixion and burial. This states that

> when he makes himself an offering for sin,
>   he shall see his offspring, he shall prolong his days;
> the will of the LORD shall prosper in his hand;
>   he shall see the fruit of the travail of his soul and be
>     satisfied...
> Therefore I will divide him a portion with the great,
>   and he shall divide the spoil with the strong;

> because he poured out his soul to death,
> and was numbered with the transgressors
>
> (Isaiah 53:10–12, RSV)

– a statement which Christ himself asserted, on the very road to Gethsemane, *must* be fulfilled in him.

It is clear, however, that the disciples, like their Jewish compatriots, did not understand these passages – or several others, such as Daniel 9:26 and Psalm 22 – as referring to the death, resurrection and exaltation of the Messiah until the risen Christ (both on the road to Emmaus and subsequently) 'opened their minds so that they could understand the Scriptures' (Luke 24:25–27 and 44–45). But what about the phrase 'on the third day'? I cannot myself understand why some scholars are so insistent on connecting the words 'according to the Scriptures' specifically with this phrase rather than with the words 'died for our sins' and 'was raised' (1 Corinthians 15:3–4). Jesus himself is reported as predicting that 'after three days' (Mark 8:31 and parallels) he would rise again, and as referring to the 'sign of the prophet Jonah' (Matthew 12:39–40); but the prophecies in the Old Testament put their sole emphasis on the Messiah's death and exaltation. So C. F. Evans' remark, that the reference to 'the third day' in the New Testament 'probably had its origin in the application of the scriptures rather than a visit of the women' to the tomb (Evans, pp.75f.), seems very wide of the mark. The evidence points much more strongly to Dodd's conclusion that this tradition 'preserves a genuine memory that on that Sunday morning his tomb was found broken open and to all appearances empty' (Dodd, *Founder*, p.167).

There is also the fact that Jesus himself, as B. B. Warfield put it, 'deliberately staked his whole claim to the credit of men upon his resurrection. When asked for a sign he pointed to this as his single and sufficient credential' (Warfield, p.537). Just as Jonah was a sign to a previous generation, he said, so would his death and resurrection transcend any and every other proof of who he was. But it is obvious that he could not have meant that this decisive proof would be provided by a purely spiritual survival of physical death and a manifestation of himself to his disciples which would be no more than that of a ghost-like apparition. He must have been referring to a resurrection of his body from the grave – transformed, no doubt, into a 'spiritual body'. Only so could he be touched, or need to tell people *not* to touch (or 'cling to') him (John 20:17).

Then again, there is the testimony of Christian experience down the ages, and the multitude of men and women – rich and poor, learned and ignorant, respectable and reprobate – who have found in the risen Christ their joy, peace and certainty. All down the centuries he has continued to say, 'Here I am! I stand at the door and knock. If anyone hears my voice and opens the door, I will go in and eat with him, and he with me' (Revelation 3:20). He still says the same today. This is not, of course, to suggest that every Christian has a vivid, mystical experience of the risen Lord; but it means that the man who counts on the resurrection, and invites the living Christ into his heart and life as Saviour and Lord, will find his faith confirmed by the inward testimony of the Holy Spirit (Romans 8:16).

Finally, there is the uniqueness of the one who rose. However natural it might seem for someone to say that, whatever the evidence, he could never believe that Tom Smith could lie for hours in a tomb and then rise from the dead, this would not apply to the central figure of the Gospels. Quite apart from the resurrection, there is excellent evidence, as we saw in chapter 2, that he was much more than *only* a man. The incredible thing, to my mind, is that such as he should ever have died 'for us men and for our salvation'. But, granted that he did die, is it really surprising that he should rise again? Could we not affirm with Peter that it was impossible that death should 'keep its hold on him' (Acts 2:24)?

## The ascension

It is clear from the New Testament as a whole that the concepts of the resurrection and exaltation of Christ go very closely together. I myself believe, with Michael Ramsey, that Jesus' 'journey to the Father' actually took place on Easter Day, as John seems to imply (John 20:17). Where else was he, during the 'forty days', in the intervals between his fairly numerous 'appearances' to his disciples? But I certainly believe that what we term 'the ascension' (as recorded in Luke 24:50–53 and, in more detail, in Acts 1:9–11) was a historical – as well as a symbolical – event at the end of the 'forty days'. In this, by his visible withdrawal of himself from his disciples' gaze, he signified to them that this sequence of appearances and almost physical fellowship was at an end, and that – until such time as he should equally visibly reappear in his Parousia – his spiritual presence and fellowship would be always and everywhere available through the Holy Spirit whose advent he had commanded them to await.

## We must take the evidence as a whole

Another point which needs stressing is that the evidence must be considered as a whole. It is comparatively easy to suggest a possible alternative explanation for one or another of the different strands which make up this testimony. But such explanations are valueless unless they fit the other strands in the testimony as well. A number of different theories, each of which might conceivably be applicable to part of the evidence but which do not themselves cohere into an intelligible pattern, can provide no alternative to the one interpretation which fits all the facts.

Lastly, it can be asserted with confidence that men and women disbelieve the Easter story not *because* of the evidence but *in spite* of it. It is not that they weigh the evidence with open minds, assess its relevance and cogency and finally decide that it is suspect or inadequate. Instead, they start with the *a priori* conviction that the resurrection of Christ would constitute such an incredible event that it could not be accepted or believed without scientific demonstration of an irrefutable nature. But it is idle to demand proof of this sort for any event in history. Historical evidence, from its very nature, can never amount to more than a very high degree of probability. It is on such evidence that virtually all our knowledge of the past depends.

Speaking of what he terms the 'Grand Miracle' of the incarnation, C. S. Lewis wrote:

If the thing happened, it was the central event in the history of the Earth – the very thing that the whole story has been about. Since it happened only once, it is by Hume's standards infinitely improbable. But then the whole history of the Earth has also happened only once; is it therefore incredible? Hence the difficulty, which weighs upon Christian and atheist alike, of estimating the probability of the Incarnation. It is like asking whether the existence of nature herself is intrinsically probable. That is why it is easier to argue, on historical grounds, that the Incarnation actually occurred than to show, on philosophical grounds, the probability of its occurrence (Lewis, *Miracles*, pp.112f.)

Our argument in this book is that the evidence for the historical basis of the Christian faith, for the essential validity of the New Testament witness to the person and teaching of Christ himself, for the fact and significance of his atoning death, and for the historicity of the empty tomb and the apostolic testimony to the resurrection, is such as to provide an adequate foundation for the venture of faith.

People often talk as though faith were some special endowment, whether to be prized above rubies or distrusted as a dangerous delusion, vouchsafed to certain types of persons; and that it has little or no connection with an intelligent appraisal of facts. This is, in my view, a grave misconception. Some people, no doubt, are more credulous than others, and to them faith may seem to come more easily than to most of us. But true faith must always have a firm basis in reason, although it must also, by its very nature, go beyond mere reason. In every department of life we act on certain logical and reasonable assumptions, but without a full understanding of all that lies behind them. We use electricity, for example, because we know what it can provide in the way of light, heat and sound, and we understand something of how it does so; but we do not fully understand the nature of electricity itself. To say that we would never switch on the light, the fire or the radio until we had attained this perfect understanding would be a sign of stupidity, not intelligence. It would certainly make life somewhat bleak!

I am convinced that, in much the same way, the foundations of the Christian faith are such that it is an act of intelligence, not credulity, deliberately to take the decisive step of self-committal to the living Christ. In the final analysis this means a person-to-person relationship which involves an outreach of our whole personality and differs fundamentally from the pursuit of historical investigation or the exercise of logical deduction. But the intellectual and the experimental are not contradictory. On the contrary, they go hand in hand, and the second confirms the first.

## What does the resurrection prove?

Most obviously, I suppose (and this is one of the chief motifs of 1 Corinthians 15), the resurrection of Jesus proves that there is a life beyond the grave for others too (1 Corinthians 15:12–19). Shakespeare's reference to a country 'from whose bourn no traveller returns' is not true, for one traveller has in fact come back from that very 'bourn', to which he has now returned 'to prepare a place' for his followers (John 14:2–3) where they will 'see his face' (Revelation 22:4), at last be 'conformed to his likeness' (Romans 8:29; Philippians 3:20–21), and share with him a life which is 'imperishable' and 'immortal' (1 Corinthians 15:52–54), in a sphere in which God will be 'all in all' (1 Corinthians 15:28).

What is even more to the point in our context, however, is that the early church clearly regarded the resurrection as the final proof that Jesus was not only the Messiah, but the 'Son of God' (Romans 1:4). The fact that the New Testament speaks of his having 'been raised' from the dead more often than of his 'rising' from the dead has been taken by some as putting the emphasis on the power of God rather than the deity of Jesus – for we believe that we shall all, one day, be so 'raised'. There can certainly be no doubt about the emphasis on the power of God; but the phrase also puts a decisive emphasis on the fact that, by this act of power, God openly acknowledged Jesus as his Son – rather than the blasphemer his Jewish critics accused him of being – and installed him as such. He was, of course, Son of God from eternity; but now he had become man, had endured human temptation and suffering, had been perfected in his human character, and had been exalted as glorified Man to the throne of the universe. No wonder his disciples now began to call him 'the Lord Jesus', to apply to him Old Testament verses which originally applied to Israel's covenant God, and to accord him worship.

The resurrection also proved the efficacy of his death on the cross. This was much more than a martyr's death, for he had 'died for our sins' (1 Corinthians 15:3), and had thus demonstrated God's love for us in the most decisive way (1 John 4:10). Now, acquitted of our sins, we can – and must – serve him here on earth, try to help others to know him and his salvation, and pray that God's own love may continually be 'poured into our hearts by the Holy Spirit, whom he has given us' (Romans 5:5).

Not only so, but his resurrection means that he is still alive – 'the same yesterday and today and for ever' (Hebrews 13:8) – reigning as our High Priest. He can understand us through and through; he can – and does – sympathize with us in our weaknesses, temptations and sufferings; and he is able to succour and save (Hebrews 4:15; 7:25). He is not only the minister of the heavenly sanctuary who brings us into living fellowship with God, but he is also the mediator of the new covenant in which his 'laws', instead of being inscribed on external tablets which challenge an unwilling (and even impossible) obedience, are written internally on our hearts and minds, so that our desires and ways of thinking are progressively transformed.

In this world we have been told not to expect an easy life, but a tough one: troubles (John 16:33), suffering (1 Peter 1:6), opposition (John 15:18) and 'trials of many kinds' (James 1:2). But we have a guarantee that 'No temptation has seized you except what is common to man. And God is faithful; he will not let you be tempted beyond what you can bear. But when you are tempted, he will also provide a way out so that you can stand up under it' (1 Corinthians 10:13). Meanwhile grace which is 'sufficient', peace which 'transcends all understanding', and even a joy 'so glorious that it cannot be described' are all available (2 Corinthians 12:9; Philippians 4:7; 1 Peter 1:8) even in the present, while our glorious future inheritance will never 'perish, spoil or fade', and we ourselves shall be protected by God's power until we reach it (1 Peter 1:4–5).

## Conclusion

Both Easter and Pentecost are of supreme significance for the Christian, the church and the world. Yet there is also a real sense in which Easter basically serves, in Zahrnt's words, to

> reveal – of course only to faith – what Jesus already was. We purposely say 'reveal' instead of 'bring out', because with the words 'bring out' there is always the fear that something alien might creep in, something which does not belong to Jesus, something 'sub-Christian', or rather something 'super-Christian', and hence thoroughly 'un-Christian'. All too often the Church in referring to the Resurrection has exaggerated Jesus so falsely that it becomes almost impossible to recognize any continuity between the earthly Jesus and the Exalted Christ, between the preaching and the preached Christ. But Jesus is no different after Easter from what he was before Easter. After his Resurrection it simply comes about that everything which earlier was indirectly and obscurely present appears in a new, bright light. Now Jesus emerges as the person he really is (Zahrnt, p.138).

This quotation brings us back once more to the matter of faith. I well remember an occasion, some years ago, when I was invited by the Rector of a church in a university city to an informal discussion, with 'no holds barred', which he held once a month for faculty members and research students. I was to speak first on the evidence for the resurrection, and then all who wished could express their views. As the discussion developed our host turned to a local professor of philosophy, not himself a Christian, and asked him if he would tell us frankly what he thought of my introductory thesis – and I can still remember the terms of his reply. 'Well,' he said, 'when Anderson was dealing with the various theories which have been put forward, down the centuries, to explain the Easter story on a rationalistic basis, I found him wholly convincing. I agree that none of them are water-tight or plausible. All I would say is that, if someone feels he cannot accept the fact of the resurrection, he will shrug his shoulders and say "Well, I can't explain it. But it simply could not have happened!"'

I asked if I might paraphrase his answer, and to this he at once agreed. 'What you have said', I replied, 'is that if someone won't accept the resurrection – or let me use your word and say "cannot" – then he won't. And that is precisely my experience. But I suggest that this will not be *because* of the evidence, but *in spite* of it' – and to this he was prepared to agree. So I said that this raised the question whether this inability (or refusal?) to believe was based exclusively on intellectual criteria, or whether a moral element was not involved – namely, a reluctance to recognize Christ as Saviour and Lord, with all that this would entail. The picture we get of Jesus in the Gospels is of one who would never perform a miracle to convince an intellectual dilettante, but was always ready to help one who really meant business.

What I would suggest to any who want to come to a firm conviction is that they should read John's Gospel with a prayer like this. 'O God' (adding, if they feel this necessary, 'if there be a God'), 'if you will show me who Jesus Christ really is as I read this book, then I am ready to follow him whole-heartedly and for ever.' Anyone could pray such a prayer with honesty, since it involves no *intellectual* presuppositions. But it involves a major *moral* presupposition: a willingness honestly to follow such light as may be given.

But why do I suggest John's Gospel? Because it is the declared purpose of this Gospel to bring men and women not only to intellectual conviction in the deity of Christ, but also to a vital experience of the new life he came to give, for towards the end of the Gospel we read:

Jesus did many other miraculous signs in the presence of his disciples, which are not recorded in this book. But these are written that you may believe that Jesus is the Christ, the Son of God, and that by believing you may have life in his name (John 20:30–31).

In the First Epistle of John we find this put in even more vivid terms to those willing to respond:

> It was there from the beginning; we have heard it; we have seen it with our own eyes; we looked upon it, and felt it with our own hands; and it is of this we tell. Our theme is the word of life. This life was made visible; we have seen it and bear our testimony; we here declare to you the eternal life which dwelt with the Father and was made visible to us . . . .
>
> The witness is this: that God has given us eternal life, and that this life is found in his Son. He who possesses the Son has life indeed; he who does not possess the Son of God has not that life.
>
> This letter is to assure you that you have eternal life. It is addressed to those who give their allegiance to the Son of God (1 John 1:1–2; 5:11–13, NEB).

Looking back over the ground covered by these chapters, it seems to me that the point from which we started – the testimony of the New Testament to the unique nature of the Christian message as it is there set forth – is clear enough. All the other world religions (together with a great deal that goes by the name of Christianity) set out to teach men how they can earn 'salvation' (however, precisely, they understand this term); how they can climb up to heaven, as it were, to discover God; how they can atone for their own past sins; or how they can make themselves one with God. But the New Testament states unequivocally that this simply cannot be done. Men and women can never earn salvation, however hard they try; they can never climb up to heaven, for the gulf is far too wide; they can never atone for the sins of the past, for they cannot even keep free from sin in the present and the future; and they can never make themselves one with a holy God.

All this is wholly beyond man's power; it cannot – and, indeed, it *need* not – be done. For it is precisely at this point that the good news of the incredible love and spontaneous initiative of God himself meets us in our need. This is the unique element in the gospel, which tells us that what we could never do, *God has done*. We cannot climb up to heaven to discover God, but God has come to earth, in the person of his Son, to reveal himself to us in the only way we could really understand: in terms of a human life. We can never atone for our sins, but God in Christ has dealt with the barrier of sin, once for all, on the cross. We can never make ourselves one with a holy God, but God in Christ offers to come and share with us his own divine and eternal life – provided we ask him to do so, as our Saviour and Lord. Nor is this wishful thinking; it is sober fact, to which many of us can testify from personal experience.

# Appendix

## The Anastasis: The Resurrection of Jesus as an Historical Event, by J. Duncan M. Derrett.

It has been suggested that the very brief reference in the text of my book to this monograph (which was all that I could feasibly insert in a script that was already in the hands of my publisher before I had seen Derrett's work) stands in need of amplification and comment. Hence this Appendix.

Derrett's 'reconstruction' is novel and distinctly idiosyncratic. As always, he brings to this study a very considerable knowledge of the Bible and Jewish *haggada,* an impressive acquaintance with a wide assortment of authors both past and contemporary, and a highly ingenious imagination (to which he has here given free rein). So I shall try both to summarize his thesis and to retain its flavour, so far as I can, by quoting his own words – together with a few passing comments.

Jesus was a vagrant 'wonder-worker' (p.76) whose 'life and work even as depicted by the Gospels was that of a recognisable human innovator and entrepreneur' (p.130). He 'seems to have identified the two characters, the Messiah and the [Suffering] Servant,[1] and played both rôles simultaneously' (p.120). 'He was pleased that Peter saw him as Son of God, because he was interested in sonship and to him sonship meant obedience, and therefore likeness' (p.121). 'In his career he has reproduced the feats of Joseph, Moses, Samson, Samuel, Elijah, Elisha, Jonah: in the obedience to death he has surpassed Isaac. Compelled by the Holy Spirit, his whole life is the working out, in banal fact, of the scriptural scenario he has envisaged.... He waits until the Jewish disease, $m^e sîrâ$ [defined at p.10 as 'denunciation of a fellow-member to outsiders to be destroyed by them'], has incubated in the Twelve, his Patriarchs of the new community, his Witnesses of the crossing of Jordan, and then he knows that all is ready. The actors have assembled, the stage is set; the curtain must go up, the drama must commence' (p.122) – and he was crucified. But although he suffered inchoate or 'clinical death' on the cross, he was buried before 'brain-death'

[1] *Cf.* J. D. M. Derrett, *Studies in the New Testament*, Vol. 2, pp.184ff. The 'Servant Songs' can be found in Isaiah 42:1–4; 49:1–6; 50:4–9; and, especially in this context, 52:13 – 53:12.

supervened (*cf.* chapters 2–5, in which Derrett discusses this subject in some detail).

Derrett follows Schenke in asserting that Mark's last [authentic] verses, 16:1–8, 'are not a historical source themselves. They are evidence of a formula for recitation at the Sepulchre, pre-Marcan, perhaps long pre-Marcan' (p.60) – and he returns to his speculations about visits to the tomb, from a *very* early date, in pages 135–138. But he emphasizes that the 'Young Man' of Mark 16, who was 'very probably an employee of Joseph' (p.52), 'is indeed a key figure in our reconstruction'; and he is 'content to view him either as the original finder of Jesus or his companion' (p.61), and Jesus' messenger both to the women and, through them, to his disciples (*cf.* p.64). 'After telling [the women] in a very unangelic idiom "not to dither"', he 'satisfies himself that they are visiting Jesus the Nazarene, "the crucified one"' – and Derrett can imagine how 'the majestic words that follow must often have been recited at the Sepulchre, with the guide's left hand pointing down at the words "He is not here" and his right forefinger upwards at "He has been raised!...observe the place where he was laid! Go, tell his pupils and Peter [i.e. not excluding Peter] that he leads you [all] into Galilee. There you shall see him, as he told you"' (p.64).

But Derrett is not prepared to take the word 'Galilee' at its face value, and continues:

> The Greek original of the English 'Galilee' is a vocalisation of a Hebrew or Aramaic cluster which would then have been written GLYL, but pronounced, according to context, *galīl* or *golēl*. It can be taken as certain that in the original it was preceded by the definite article, 'the GLYL'.... What this amounts to is that the disciples' meeting place with their Lord, the trysting-place, as it were, is 'GLYL'. Imagination must now get to work to establish what GLYL means. What implications were legitimate, and what not? Fancy could do wonders with that word, and the fact that there was such concentration upon it suggests powerfully that Jesus himself gave them practically no help. If so, *we can easily guess why*. The authentic message of the Risen One must be squeezed dry of every drop of meaning, because there was so little else to which they could apply their minds. About that 'GLYL's' relevance to the disciples there was no doubt but it was as *cryptic* as the Last Words (p.65. His italics).

This revival from inchoate death cannot, Derrett concedes, 'have been planned by Jesus himself, but when it occurred he knew what it was' (p.122), as would 'anyone who had been obsessed with the principle [of vicarious suffering] inherent in Is. 52–53, and had actually worked the thing out to the death'.... So, it 'seems Jesus realised that the corner-stone had been fitted in the arch' (p.123).

Derrett's own 'guess is that as strangers buried him so strangers took care of him', and this 'left Jesus free to communicate in quite a new tone with his former table-companions.... They were his partners, but in the sense of being bagmen: he supplied the capital and they were to go about selling his stock' (p.92).

Before the Anastasis 'Jesus could tell by a sufferer's readiness for charismatic cure that God had forgiven his sins, and Jesus confirms by his act of healing that that is what has happened (since people believed at that time that sickness was the result of sin). But after the Anastasis all is changed. The divine power of forgiveness has been irrevocably entrusted to Jesus, and is delegated by him to his apostles. How has this come about?' (p.123).

A few pages earlier, Derrett had summarized his understanding of the Jewish concepts of atonement and expiation: 'The idea was simple. A person with relatively few sins could offer his own suffering...to expiate vicariously the sins of others. Older than Christianity, the notion is fully outlined in 4 Maccabees' (p.118). So now he applies this to 'the theology of the Anastasis' in these words (p.123): 'Let us assume that a person who is a sinner accepts his own death as an atonement. He is entitled to inherit the World to Come' (a proposition which Derrett bases on what is, with respect, a wholly mistaken understanding of 1 Corinthians 5:5). Then he proceeds:

> Let us assume that a person who is sinless suffers and dies without fault on his part: he accumulates merit thereby, and those that love him (i.e. are in solidarity with him) can share that merit if that is his intention, and benefit from the removal of their sins from the account, as it were. Let us imagine that a sinless person voluntarily accepts great suffering, including death, on behalf of others, *and is restored to life*. It is obvious that God has accepted his suffering, but, by not accepting his life as forfeit, 'justified' him. By his further suffering and death he accumulates, being *ex hypothesi* entirely sinless, an infinity of merit; and by allowing persons nominated by himself or his agents to share his spiritual condition bestows sinlessness upon them (provided they abide by the conditions of the relationship, of course – as indicated at Mt. 18:27, 31–34). This is a divine quality, and by his Anastasis Jesus acquired that. Not only can God forgive sins, but the risen Christ, who did not have that power in any logical sense previously, now acquires it. He delegates the power, and this gives his teaching a special edge it did not have before (p.123).

This exposition leaves me gasping. It is flawed *ab initio*, with respect, by the fact that Derrett appears to have completely overlooked two basic principles in the Old Testament. First, the Psalmist insists that 'No *man* can redeem the life of another or give to God a ransom for him – the ransom for a life is costly, no [human] payment is ever enough' (Psalm 49:7–8. My italics). Secondly, the prophet Ezekiel makes the categorical statement that 'The soul who sins is the one who will die. The son will not share the guilt of the father, nor will the father share the guilt of the son. The righteousness of the righteous man will be credited to *him*, and the wickedness of the wicked will be charged against *him*' (Ezekiel 18:20. My italics). It would be nothing short of gross injustice for a human judge to allow an innocent man to die in the place of the guilty, and God would never be a party to such a travesty of justice. The forgiveness of sins is, as Derrett states, a 'divine quality' and the 'ransom' and 'expiation' which only the death of Jesus on the cross could provide owed its efficacy not *primarily* to his sinlessness (although that, too, was essential) but to the fact that, although truly human, he was truly God-in-manhood. The 'divine quality' to which Derrett refers was not 'acquired' by his death, but gave that death its unique quality and efficacy – just as his resurrection did not *make* him 'Son of God', but 'declared with power' what he had in fact always been, even when 'crucified in weakness' (Romans 1:4; 2 Corinthians 13:4).

We must return to Derrett's thesis. 'How', he asks, 'did Jesus commission [his disciples]?' 'Possibly by visiting them in his own time, by some appropriate conveyance, speaking perhaps very little, but placing his hands, whose wrists bore the mark of the nails (Lk. 24:39, Jn. 20:20), on their heads.... The laying on of hands conveys the Spirit, without which their morale would have been low, and their efforts vain.' It seems clear, Derrett states, that Christians 'apparently believed that Jesus exercised the divine power *after his ascension*'...although 'No other person "risen" from death has been worshipped as God! No precedent, therefore, existed: nor has any other example occurred since! The silence is so loud, it cries out for a conjecture, and one is to hand' (p.96). So Derrett feels 'entitled to tender what follows with all deference as a mere conjecture' (p.97).

'The disciples, fearing that his body might have been reanimated by an evil spirit or the spirit of some predeceased, disembodied person (Mk. 6:49, Lk. 24:37; cf. Mk. 6:14: Herod had such a notion of 'reincarnation'), *could* have asked, trembling, "Lord (a polite form of address), who are you? (Mt. 14:28, Jn. 21:12, Acts 9:5 par). He *could* have replied in Hebrew..."I am that I am".... This dual formula was the ineffable Name by which God identified himself for Moses in a passage which only Mark amongst the evangelists takes the trouble to point out to us. Jesus himself (Mk. 12:26) calls attention to the "passage of the Bush" in connection with the resurrection... The simple expression in Greek, *egō eimi*, which can be unthinkingly translated "Here I am", or "It is I", is a magic formula, a veritable theophany.... If he did utter this formula, exactly appropriate to one who despatched apostles as messengers from God, it would take care of our problem without residue: and, for those actually present on the occasion, would settle not only their doubts, but also their future' (p.97).

His sufferings had, however, been such that 'brain-death' must soon have intervened. So the disciples would have been faced with the problem of what to do with the body – since Derrett insists that 'the Ascension is a euphemism, filling a vacuum on the analogy of...the Patriarchs, Elijah (2 Kings 2:1, 11–12) and...Moses' (p.90). He also is at pains to point out several objections to the re-burial of the body and insists that 'the case for the unexpected alternative, cremation, is strong' – relying greatly, in this connection, on the 'Aqêdâ (binding) of Isaac and the burning of the ram that 'stood in for him' as a 'holocaust (a whole offering)', and also 'the biblical requirement that the paschal lamb [or, rather, so much of it as had not been eaten!] should be cremated (1 Cor. 5:7)' (pp.81f.).

'Did Jesus authorise it? Fathers of the early Church later saw the crucifixion as foreshadowed by the sacrifice of Isaac. As early as the Talpioth ossuaries [dating back to *very* early in the Christian era (cf.

pp.124ff.)] a cross of faggots implied the resurrection.... In the disposal of his own body Jesus would, of course, after his Anastasis, have full authority. Jesus did not call his disciples to him, he went to them, preserving his initiative to the last. Did he tell them to do with him "as with Isaac"? That was all that was necessary' (p.83).

So the 'men of Galilee', as Derrett imagines them, took upon themselves the extraordinary task of cremating their Master (p.85) – and he infers that this was done by night (when there must have been thousands of bonfires at Passover) and that the ashes and any bones not consumed by the fire were deposited at the chief of three 'Places of Burning' – the Place 'in the Kedron Valley, right against the Temple wall which was also the City wall. Down that Valley came periodically torrents of rain-water.... The Passover lamb is also a sacrifice, and is therefore appropriately disposed of there. Any ashes deposited by a priest, or, in the case of the day after Passover, by a lay Israelite, on the heap at the principal Place of Burning will have gone absolutely unnoticed and no embarrassment would be caused to anyone' (pp.85f.)

'My own impression', he writes, 'is that Jesus did visit his disciples, and ate and drank with them –though not *necessarily* more than once' (p.109). But the post-resurrection appearances recorded in the Gospels, he asserts, 'were written to fill a vacuum and to satisfy curiosity', although this 'does not mean that they did not correspond in some minimal measure to facts' (p.108).... 'But as soon as rumours of his survival reached those who loved him...a rush of reports of visions coming in...met ripples of reassurance from the capital spreading outward that Jesus was actually setting his business in motion' (p.109, whatever that may mean). Derrett also insists that 'the appearances convey nothing whatever about Jesus's teaching which is not available to us from stories located *before* the Crucifixion' (p.108).

That any such speculative suggestions as these – in parts purely conjectural by admission, and in parts quite astonishingly dogmatic – represent a positive travesty of the Christian faith, is the argument of my book as a whole; so I shall not repeat what I have already written. But there are a few points about *The Anastasis* which demand special comment.

1. It is obvious, both from the title of Derrett's book (together with the author's initial explanation) and from its total contents, that he insists on consistently translating the noun *anastasis* and the corresponding verb, wherever they occur, as 'getting up' or 'waking up' rather than 'resurrection', 'raising up' or 'being raised'. Either translation is, of course, perfectly permissible, so the choice depends on the context (and the concept of 'sleep' is frequently used in the Bible as a synonym for 'death'). But the New Testament, more often than not, uses a different verb (*egeirō*), either in the active voice, in phrases such as 'God raised him (Jesus) up', or in the passive, 'he was raised'. Derrett insists that *anastasis* is not only the literal, but the 'original and correct name', for Jesus' experience '*even if he, for reasons of his own, wished to profit from such a confusion* (p.2. His italics). But in point of fact the verb *egeirō* is used in our earliest sources (*e.g.* Galatians 1:1; 1 Thessalonians 1:10; 1 Corinthians 6:14 and 15:4, 12–17; Mark 14:28; *etc.*). Derrett asserts that this represents 'theological brigandage', and suspects 'that it was Jesus's

own idea'(p.2). It is significant in this context that he takes Mark, to whose Gospel he ascribes a very early date (p.10), rather than 1 Corinthians 15:1–11, as 'our prime source on Jesus's Resurrection' (p.xi); that he asserts that a 'tradition to handle the Resurrection in a tangential way starts at least as early as Paul, who is supremely uninterested in it as an experience undergone by Jesus' (*sic*, p.x)[2]; and that he insists that 'Paul's baroque theology will have presupposed the use of a sober "narrative" in liturgy well within his own life time', p.10). What he does *not* make clear is that his 'reconstruction' in effect gives the lie to the apostolic proclamation in its basic essentials - based as this was, from the first, on Jesus' atoning death on the cross, on his triumphant resurrection as Lord of life, and the seal of the Holy Spirit on their commission to preach this.

2. It is surely obvious that all this would imply what can only be described as a deliberate conspiracy of silence, or of a radically 'doctored' message, on the part of Peter, James and the 'Twelve' as a whole, to say nothing of Paul. Not only so, but some of Derrett's asides (if this term can legitimately be used of words sometimes printed in italics) suggest that Jesus himself was both conscious and willing that something like this perversion of the facts would be likely to result. How else can one understand remarks such as *'even if he, for reasons of his own, wished to profit from such a confusion'*? Other examples of somewhat similar innuendoes could be quoted (*cf.* p.2).

3. Derrett's treatment of 1 Corinthians 15:1–11 (together with Paul's argument in the rest of that chapter, in Philippians 3:20f. and many other passages) is totally inadequate. Like many other scholars who develop an 'idée fixe', he accepts the testimony of the New Testament when it suits him, and discards (or even derides) it when it does not, in what appears to be a wholly arbitrary way.

4. It can scarcely be denied that the New Testament as a whole throbs with the experience of a risen and exalted Lord, whom the apostles (and other disciples) felt free to worship, to address in prayer, and to associate with Old Testament verses which clearly applied, in their original setting, to Israel's covenant God. They also consistently coupled together their 'one God, the Father' and their 'one Lord, Jesus Christ' (1 Corinthians 8:6), while the book of Revelation continually refers, in one phrase or another, to 'the throne of God and of the Lamb'.

5. Like all varieties of the 'swoon theory', Derrett's 'reconstruction' runs up against Strauss's trenchant criticism, quoted on pp.85f., above: 'It is impossible that a being who had stolen half dead out of the sepulchre...weak and ill [and who, on Derrett's theory, very soon suffered brain death and was cremated] could have given the disciples the impression that he was a Conqueror over death and the grave, the Prince of life, an impression which lay at the bottom of their future ministry.'

6. Derrett's primary purpose, it seems clear, is to give a credible explanation of how the death of Jesus could be regarded as in *some* sense (however inadequate) an atonement for the sins of others; how the apostles could have felt able to testify that he had (again in *some* sense) risen from the tomb; and how it would be possible to explain the

[2]But *cf.* Philippians 3:10f., 20f.

disappearance of his body – while still declining to regard him as more than a very great, but exclusively human, being. This would, however, not only invalidate the apostolic proclamation, but evacuate his death and resurrection of their saving power – and that, not because this 'reconstruction' is supported by the evidence, but in spite of the fact that the evidence points decisively against it.

# Bibliography

(*This is not a reading list, but is confined to books and articles quoted or cited in this book.*)

Allegro, J. M., *The Sacred Mushroom and the Cross* (Hodder, London, 1973).
—— *Search in the Desert* (W. H. Allen, London, 1965).
Anderson, Norman, *A Lawyer among the Theologians* (Hodder, London, 1973).
—— *The Mystery of the Incarnation* (Hodder, London, 1977).
—— *The Teaching of Jesus* (Hodder, London, 1983).
Atkinson, James, 'Atonement', in *A Dictionary of Christian Theology* (ed. Alan Richardson. SCM, London, 1969).
Aulén, Gustaf, *Christus Victor* (E. T., SPCK, London, 1931).
Ballard, Frank, *The Miracles of Unbelief* (T. and T. Clark, Edinburgh, 1904).
Betz, Otto, *What do we know about Jesus?* (E. T., SCM, London, 1968).
Blaiklock, E. M., *Layman's Answer* (Hodder, London, 1968).
Bornkamm, Günther, *Jesus of Nazareth* (E. T., Hodder, London, 1960).
Bouyer, Louis, *Le Fils éternel: Théologie de la Parole de Dieu et Christologie* (Cerf, Paris, 1974), quoted in English in E. L. Mascall, *Theology and the Gospel of Christ* (SPCK, London, 1977).
Bultmann, Rudolf, *Jesus and the Word* (E. T., Collins Fontana, London, 1958).
Caird, G. B., *The Gospel of Luke* (Penguin, Harmondsworth, 1963).
Campenhausen, Hans von, 'The Events of Easter and the Empty Tomb', in his *Tradition and Life in the Church* (E. T., Collins, London, 1968).
Carson, D. A., *Commentary on Matthew* (Zondervan, Grand Rapids, 1984).
—— (ed.), *From Sabbath to Lord's Day* (Zondervan, Grand Rapids; Paternoster, Exeter, 1982).
Cowper, B. Harris, *The Apocryphal Gospels and other Documents relating to the History of Christ*, 3rd ed. revised (Williams and Norgate, London, 1870).

Cranfield, C. E. B., *The Gospel according to St Mark* (CUP, Cambridge, 1959).

Cullmann, Oscar, *The Theology of the New Testament* (E. T., SCM, London, 1959).

Daube, David, *The New Testament and Rabbinic Judaism* (Athlone Press, London, 1956).

Derrett, J. Duncan M., *The Anastasis: The Resurrection of Jesus as an Historical Event* (Drinkwater, Shipston-on-Stour, 1982).

Dodd, C. H., *The Founder of Christianity* (Collins, London, 1971).

—— 'The Historical Problem of the Death of Jesus', in his *More New Testament Studies* (Manchester University Press, Manchester, 1968).

Dunkerley, Roderic, *Beyond the Gospels* (Penguin, Harmondsworth, 1957).

Evans, C. F., *The Resurrection and the New Testament* (SCM, London, 1970).

Forsyth, P. T., *The Work of Christ* (Hodder, London, 1910).

Frazer, James G., *The Golden Bough* (Macmillan, London, 1913).

Galot, J., *La Personne du Christ* (Duculot, Gambloux et Lethielleux, Paris, 1969), quoted in English in E.-L. Mascall, *Theology and the Gospel of Christ* (SPCK, London, 1977).

Goethe, J. W. von, *Conversations with Eckerman* (iii), quoted in English in Ballard (*q.v.*).

Green, Michael, *World on the Run* (IVP, Leicester, 1983).

Hanson, R. P. C., 'Enterprise of Emancipating Christian Belief from History', in A. T. Hanson (ed.), *Vindications: Essays on the historical basis of Christianity* (SCM, London, 1966).

Harvey, A. E. (ed.), *God Incarnate: Story and Belief* (SPCK, London, 1981).

Howe, W. D., *Selections from William Hazlitt* (Ginn, Boston, 1913).

Hughes, H. Maldwyn, *What is the Atonement?* (James Clarke, London, n.d.).

Hunter, A. M., *Paul and his Predecessors,* Revised ed. (SCM, London, 1961).

Jefferson, C. E., *The Character of Jesus* (Grosset and Dunlap, New York, 1936).

Jenkins, D. E. and Caird, G. B., *Jesus and God* (Faith Press, London, 1965).

Käsemann, E., *Essays on New Testament Themes* (E. T., SCM, London, 1960).

Klausner, Joseph, *Jesus of Nazareth* (George Allen and Unwin, London, 1925).

Kümmel, W. G., *Promise and Fulfilment* (E. T., SCM, London, 1957).

Künneth, Walter, *The Theology of the Resurrection* (E. T., SCM, London, 1965).

Ladd, G. E., *The Presence of the Future* (Eerdmans, Grand Rapids, 1974; SPCK, London, 1981).

Lake, Kirsopp, *The Historical Evidence for the Resurrection of Christ* (Williams and Norgate, London, 1907).

Lecky, W. E. H., *History of European Morals from Augustus to Charlemagne*

(Longmans Green, London, 1877).

Lewis, C. S., *Mere Christianity* (Collins Fontana, London, 1970).

—— *Miracles* (Collins Fontana, London, 1960).

Liddon, H. P., *The Divinity of Our Lord and Saviour Jesus Christ* (Rivingtons, London, 1889).

Manson, T. W., 'The Cleansing of the Temple', in *Bulletin of the John Rylands Library* **33**, 1951.

Marsh, John, *Saint John* (Penguin, Harmondsworth, 1963; SCM, London, 1968).

Mill, John Stuart, *Three Essays on Religion,* 4th ed. (Longmans Green, London, 1875).

Milligan, W., *The Resurrection of our Lord* (Macmillan, New York, 1899).

Morgan, G. Campbell, *The Crises of the Christ* (Pickering and Inglis, London, 1945).

Morison, Frank, *Who Moved the Stone?* (Faber and Faber, London, 1958).

Morris, Leon, *Glory in the Cross* (Hodder, London, 1966).

Moule, C. F. D., *The Origin of Christology* (CUP, Cambridge, 1977).

—— *The Phenomenon of the New Testament* (SCM, London, 1967).

Neill, Stephen C., *Christian Faith and Other Faiths* (OUP, Oxford, 1961).

—— *The Interpretation of the New Testament 1861–1961* (OUP, Oxford, 1966).

Nicoll, W. Robertson, *The Church's One Foundation* (Hodder, London, 1901).

Nineham, D. E., *The Gospel of St Mark,* Revised ed. (Adam and Charles Black, London, 1968).

Orr, James, *The Christian View of God and the World* (Andrew Elliot, Edinburgh, 1908).

—— *The Resurrection of Jesus* (Hodder, London, 1909).

Pannenberg, Wolfhart, *Jesus: God and Man* (E. T., SCM, London, 1968).

Phillips, J. B., *The Ring of Truth* (Hodder, London, 1967).

Ramsey, A. M., *God, Christ and the World* (SCM, London, 1969).

—— *The Resurrection* (Collins Fontana, London, 1961).

Rashdall, Hastings, *The Idea of Atonement in Christian Theology* (Macmillan, London, 1919).

Renan, Joseph Ernest, *Étude d'histoire religieuse,* quoted in English in Ballard (*q.v.*).

Richardson, Alan, 'Virgin Birth', in Alan Richardson (ed.), *A Dictionary of Christian Theology* (SCM, London, 1969).

Rousseau, Jean-Jacques, *Émile,* quoted in English in Ballard (*q.v.*).

Russell, Bertrand, *Why I am not a Christian* (Allen and Unwin, London, 1957).

Schaeffer, Francis A., *The God Who is There* (Hodder, London, 1968).

Schonfield, Hugh J., *The Passover Plot* (Hutchinson, London, 1965).

Selwyn, E. G., *The First Epistle of Peter* (Macmillan, London, 1947).

Shams, J. D., *Where did Jesus die?* (Lahore, 1945).

Sherwin-White, A. N., *Roman Society and Roman Law in the New Testament* (OUP, Oxford, 1963).

Simpson, P. Carnegie, *The Fact of Christ* (James Clarke, London, 1952).

Strauss, D. F., *Life of Jesus,* People's ed. (Williams and Norgate, London, 1864).

Suetonius, *Life of Claudius*. See C. K. Barrett (ed.), *The New Testament Background: Selected Documents* (SPCK, London, 1957).

Tasker, R. V. G., *The Gospel according to St Matthew* (Tyndale Press, London, 1961).

Taylor, Vincent, *The Atonement in New Testament Teaching*, 2nd ed. (Epworth Press, London, 1945).

—— *Forgiveness and Reconciliation* (Macmillan, London, 1941).

—— *Jesus and his Sacrifice* (Macmillan, London, 1937).

Temple, William, *Readings in St John's Gospel* (Macmillan, London, 1942).

Thomas, W. H. Griffith, *Christianity is Christ* (Longmans Green, London, 1925).

Vermes, Geza, 'The Gospels without Christology', in A. E. Harvey (ed.), *God Incarnate: Story and Belief* (SPCK, London, 1981).

Warfield, B. B., *The Person and Work of Christ* (Presbyterian and Reformed Publishing Co., Philadelphia, 1950).

Wenham, John, *Easter Enigma* (Paternoster, Exeter, 1984).

Zahrnt, Heinz, *The Historical Jesus* (E. T., Collins, London, 1963).

## Versions of the Bible

| | |
|---|---|
| AV | Authorized Version (King James), 1611. |
| GNB | Good News Bible, 1976. |
| JB | Jerusalem Bible, 1966. |
| JBP | J. B. Phillips, 1947–57. |
| NEB | New English Bible, 1961–70. |
| RSV | Revised Standard Version, 1946–52. |

# Index of biblical references

# Index of authors

# General index